**Peaky Blinders: Series 1-4 Episo**

GW01080067

# By JAMES DONAGHY

## Introduction

The fourth series of Peaky Blinders ushers in grandstanding camel-nosed prick Luca Changretta, a man whose lust for vengeance is as big as his snozz and that my friends is significant. He is just the latest antagonist to bump up against implausibly handsome mentalloid Tommy Shelby and his crew of razor wielding thugs. Changretta has come to avenge the deaths of his fat father and idiot brother and nothing but the complete eradication of the Shelby clan followed by a sturdy helping of faggots and peas will satisfy him.

As the Shelbys go to the mattresses facing annihilation, they do so against a backdrop of industrial turmoil as communist psychopaths attempt to enforce their sick "living wage" philosophy.

Death, heartbreak and betrayal are constant companions as we charge through a tumultuous 1926. The 20s may be roaring but so are the Shelbys, the Mafia and the British Labour Movement.

## About James Donaghy

James has been writing professionally about TV since 2006. He has written for The Guardian, The Observer, Shortlist, FHM, House, Arena and Vanity Fair Italia. He runs things at the **Aerial Telly** YouTube channel and lives and works in Birmingham.

## Praise for James Donaghy's Television Can Blow Me series

"If you can cope with weapons-grade level swearing, it is sit-and-weep-and-shake funny."

**Mhairi McFarlane**, bestselling author of **You Had Me at Hello**

"As controversial, outrageous and scathingly witty as we all secretly want to be."

**Andy Conway**, screenwriter

"Entertaining and outrageous."

**Amy Edelman, IndieReader.com**

# CONTENTS

## Series 1

## Series 2

## Series 3

## Series 4

# Series 1 Episode 1 | Sing for the moment

## Living on a frère

I see Birmingham hasn't changed much. Peaky Blinders takes us to 1919, a distant yet eerily familiar second city where Noses lurk in dark hovels, wastrels rut in the streets and you can't get a bet on without breaking the law. The Peaky Blinders gang run bookies, protection rackets and general petty scrotery in the city and pretty much nobody effs with them. The rozzers consider Arthur Shelby (Paul Anderson) the nominal leader of the crew but it's younger brother Tommoi (Cillian Murphy) who has the vision thing and the real power. Arthur is a colossally thick bag of shit which has somewhat eased Tommoi's transition to the top.

## Race war

And now look at him bidding a Chinese washerwoman blow magic dust on Monaghan Boy, a racehorse as black as soot and as feckless as a Geldof. The great thing about horseracing though is that while horses are pretty incorruptible jockeys and trainers are as bent as a nag's back leg. Tommoi will be fiddling with race results to ramp up Monaghan Boy's odds and make a killing from the bemused West Midlands underclass. That's just how he rolls.

The Blinders have fingers in many pies in fact. When the crew accidentally steal a shipment of arms the smart thing to do is to anonymously dump it for the police to find. Bookies and protection are one level but felons arming themselves with stolen artillery gets filed under *hell naw*. But the audacious thing to do is to hold onto them and charge the police to get them back. Tommoi opts for the latter course. He's a renegade future Hall of Famer this one.

Much like his old Army pal Freddie Thorn (Iddo Goldberg). Freddie may drink mild but his political views are anything but. The union firebrand is a foul pinko who is looking to fuck the power structure like he's fucking Tommoi's sister Ada (Sophie Rundle) – secretly, comprehensively and as often as possible. I can't imagine that going down well when the inevitable reveal comes. There's big deep history between the boys and not just from round Birmingham way.

"You know," he tells Tommoi "There are days when I hear about the cuttings and beatings that I really wish I'd let you take that bullet in France."

"Believe me," says Tommoi honestly "There are nights I wish you had."

### Danny boy

Another pal of theirs from the Great War lurches into The Garrison, Small Heath knocking over tables, sending pints flying and generally making a nuisance of himself. Danny Whizz-Bang is no feckless boozehound but the menkle in him is strong. An overdose of Kraut artillery turned him into a PTSD addled turd. You can't talk any sense into this wackjob, something an innocent Italian cafe owner discovers when he remonstrates with him and gets a knife in the guts for his trouble. The guinea's subsequent death leave the Italian mob baying for Danny's blood. It's just one more problem on Tommoi's pile.

## Orange is not the only brute

But wait, a new broom sweeps its way towards Birmingham. Chief Inspector Chester Campbell (Sam Neill) is a proud Protestant Ulsterman sent to the city by Minister for War and Air Winston Churchill (Andy Nyman) to solve the arms robbery. Campballs however sees it also as a holy mission to clean the city up and save it from its "three-headed beast". Bloody hell, no need to talk about Fuzzbox like that.

Oh wait, he's talking about the Fenians, the Communists and the gangs. Fair enough. He brings with him some Shankill Road thugs to whip the hopelessly corrupt Birmingham police into shape. "You are worse than them!" he barks pointing at imaginary villains, Marxists and Taigs. It's clear from his Paisleyite rhetoric that he's not fucking about.

Something Arthur finds out on a visit to the cinema. He is apprehended by Campballs' goons just as two whores are about to administer a mouth organ duet blowjob (could you have picked a worse time Constable Cuntbubble?) He gets dragged out then beaten to feck by them and after a bit of light torture Campballs proposes they can help each other. That sounds better than having his knackers stomped on again. Arthur is all ears and not just because he resembles a Toby jug looking at itself in the mirror.

Campballs wants the Peaky Blinders to be his eyes and ears, to inform him of the movements and actions of the Fenians and Communists. It's merely two years since the Russian Revolution and any monarchy that doesn't feel threatened by the masses has sorely misunderstood the situation. Campballs will not abide each-way spivs, Bolshevism or Roman Popery in the city of Birmingham. He'd probably want to keep out of Digbeth then.

## Is it a bird? Yes. Yes, it is.

To aid his quest he has his agent Grace Burgess (Annabelle Wallis) working undercover as a barmaid in The Garrison. It's a Blinders stronghold and when she turns up looking for work it's hard not to notice that she is sexually attractive.

Still, it's a rigourous interview process that involves a punishing X Factor style sing off. "In Ireland my singing made them cry and stopped them fighting," she assures the landlord although when she starts warbling it's clear that only the first half of that sentence is true.

Despite stinking the joint out with her caterwauling it turns out that Grace is *still* sexually attractive so she lands the gig. It is settled. She will sing Carrickfergus while emptying out slop buckets, punching West Brom fans in the tits and gathering information on the Peakoi Bloinders for Campballs. She's going to be a busy girl. And if her bartending's as bad as her singing a quickly unemployed one.

"That the IRA murdered my father will not affect my judgment," she tells Campballs in an emotional exposition dump. Yeah alright we get it doll. You're vengeful, conflicted and dangerous. Just please, no more singing.

## Wop justice

Having stalled for as long as was seemly, Tommoi has to carry out the death sentence on Danny Whizz-Bang. As two guineas watch with satisfaction Tommoi shoots Danny in the head like BLAAAW! and there are brains everywhere. The soppy twat falls onto a waiting barge that Uncle Charlie pilots away. Shortly afterwards, in the safety of a canal tunnel Danny comes round. He thinks he's in heaven but the truth is that Tommoi shot him with a shell filled with sheep brains to fool the Italians. He'll be heading down to London to complete a special mission. Any organised criminal conspiracy ultimately depends upon effective delegation and when a job needs doing exactly what you want is an emotionally crippled menkle on the case. Let the gangsterism begin!

## Notes and observations

- It's a powerful, promising opener and Cillian Murphy's Tommoi offers an impressive British answer to Boardwalk Empire's James Darmody – a handsome, whip-smart gangster, PTSDed to shit, all fucked up by the war.

- "The crown of a prince." Freddie, admiring the razor blade sewn into Tommoi's cap - the signature Peaky Blinder accessory.

- You may recognise dub poet Benjamin Zephaniah as slum preacher Jeremiah Jesus running his mouth about fornication as Campballs gets his first glimpse of inner-city Birmingham.

- Tommoi gets whacked out on opium to kill the memories of the war. No drug has yet been discovered though that blots out Grace's singing.

- "Are you a whore? Because if you're not, you're in the wrong place." Tommoi marks Grace's card about The Garrison early on.

# Series 1 Episode 2 | Lickey boom boom down

### Horse sense

In last week's show we discovered how many of the inhabitants of 1919 Birmingham believed themselves to be Scousers and spoke accordingly, soft lad. After his eventful introduction to the city Captain Cuntface wants to meet Tommoi at the Lickey Tea Rooms and why wouldn't he? It's a lovely little place. As added incentive he raids every pub in Birmingham under the Blinders' protection with the noteworthy exception of The Garrison. Wouldn't want Secret Agent Grace getting her fanny hairs singed when they light that place up.

Tommoi though has other priorities. He and his brothers meet up with the Gypsy Lee family to quite literally do some horsetrading. Once he's purchased the nag he starts getting salty with them and it seems like there's history there. The Gypsies respond by calling his mother a hooer and in an instant it's ON. The Shelby boys pile in with fists and boots and the slashing of razor caps. The Lees are no match for their Small Heath fury and they crumble in a shitheap on the ground. Oh they won't forget that in a hurry. A literal bullet with his literal name on confirms it. It's war between them. *Tommoi, woi must yow always gow to war? Is it because of whar 'appened in the war?*

## Family panning

Yeah, good chance. Before his tea meeting with Tommoi, Chief Inspector Campballs starts work on the second head of his three headed beast and begins rounding up the pinkos. Freddie is just done slipping Ada a length as they arrive and while they both escape before the rozzers enter it's clear that it's no longer safe for Freddie here so he's Audi 5000 while Ada gets sanctuary from a neighbour.

Early morning *copper interruptus* is the least of Ada's problems – homegirl's pregnant. They may be the worst scum Birmingham has to offer but premarital sex for women remains a sacred taboo in the Shelby family. The important thing is that nobody finds out who the father is.

"Freddie fucking Thorn!" she shouts when the family asks her "Oose is it loike?" Way to protect your boy, Ada. Tommoi sees no life for Ada with a man on the run and you know the Shelbys – very pro-life.

## Feel the burn

Pro-monarchy too and to demonstrate this they start a bonfire of portraits of the King. Tommoi tells a dopey local journalist it is a symbolic act of Kinglove agin Chief Inspector Campballs for his disgusting acts against the good criminal folk of Birmingham. They went through hell at the Somme, Tommoi says, and by committing treason, insurrection and arson they - I'll be honest I stopped listening at this point. Tommoi is a colossal bullshitter. I can tell you this much: when news of the bonfire reaches him Churchill is not happy. And when Churchill is not happy he makes damn sure that Campballs quickly shares his mood.

I'll tell you who else isn't happy. Billy Kimber, leader of the Birmingham Boys outfit and controller of the racetracks

shows up hella cranky about the Monaghan Boy fix –
suspicious betting that goes on without his sanction he takes
as an affront.

"You fucking Gypsy scum what live off the war pensions of
these poor old Garrison Lane widows!" he shouts referring to
a scam that the Blinders had not yet considered. Tommoi
gratefully makes a note "Fuck over the widows on Garrison
Lane. Get some milk while there."

Kimber's fixing to kill all the Shelbys but Tommoi suggests
another route. They have a common enemy in the Lees and
Tommoi can squash them like they was nuthin' bab. Kimber
is contemptuous but he's caught a little offguard and his
assistant tells Tommoi they can parlay more at Cheltenham
races.

**Welshing on the deal**

Campballs meanwhile hits the pubs who pay protection to
the Blinders to get Tommoi's attention as a way of
reminding him about their tea date. Tommoi seeks a date of
his own with Secret Agent Grace. He'd like to take her ~~up
the pipe repeatedly~~ to the races and early indications are that
she'd be susceptible to that. She sings him a sad song and it's
over – he's cuntstruck. He lost his heart to a Galway Girl.

So he must surely know how Freddie and Ada feel? Love,
real love? Well kind of. He may have saved his life in France
but that doesn't give him free licence to put his cock in his
sister. He tells Freddie: get the skank out of town and into
Cardiff to avoid the shame. A new life in Wales is a better
result for Freddie than he might have expected but he isn't
afraid of no Tommoi Shelby and is going to stay right here in
putrid Birmingham like the dumb communist weasel he is.

## Tea for tut

And so we arrive at the Lickey Tea Rooms for the big showdown. Tommoi bursts in demanding the finest wines available to humanity and is visibly deflated when no one gets the reference. Once they get down to business Campballs is worried about him being in bed with the Reds like Ada but Tommoi is keen not to be distracted. He wants Campballs to let his business run and expand into the race tracks. In return, he'll give him his guns back.

Well, that would get Churchill off his back. If he disagrees Tommoi assures him he'll send the guns to Belfast and the IRA. Campballs agrees but he doesn't shake on it because he has his fingers crossed. He tells Secret Agent Grace to do everything in her power to find the guns and I'm pretty certain that means letting Tommoi put his cock in her. If that stops her singing everybody wins.

### Notes and observations

- Tommoi may have ambition, street smarts and native cunning but he clearly has a blind spot where it comes to pum-pum. He falls for Grace as she sings him The Black Velvet Band, a song about a woman planting stolen goods on a man and getting him sent to a penal colony. It's called foreshadowing old boy. She even helps out with "I warn you, I'll break your heart," but it's far too late.

- "The baby's a bastard, you're a whore, but there's no word for the man who doesn't come back." Proto-feminist Aunt Pol speaking real words to Ada.

- It hasn't taken Campballs long to figure out that Tommoi is the real head of the operation which is a good job because torturing Arthur for what he knows is thin gruel indeed.

- "Now why would I shake the hand of a man who didn't even fight for his country?" Tommoi sticking it hard to Campballs for his draft dodging.

- The accents are still dicey and there's the odd cornball line but it looks terrific, comes with a banging soundtrack and has got a strut and flourish about it not usually associated with the city of Birmingham. It is a dark and unforgiving place but it KO1 whatever shitbox you're currently embarrassing yourself in.

# Series 1 Episode 3 | Look out Tommoi, he's Irish!

### In the Micks

Previously on Peaky Blinders: Birmingham isn't just there for the nasty things in life like Black Sabbath, Islamist terrorist cells and brutalist architecture. It's there for the nice things too like protection rackets, communist agitators and post-war illegal gambling. As we begin this week, two gentlemen of Ireland approach Tommoi in The Garrison for a sitdown.

"It takes a lot for a man from Sparkbrook to step inside here" says one.

It takes a lot for a man from Sparkbrook to step anywhere. The Irishmen have heard things – things about guns. Being representatives of the Irish Republican Army they have a natural interest in such tales of illegally acquired guns – would Tommoi know anything about that, to be sure? Tommoi stonewalls and it pisses one of the Micks, the drunkard Maguire, right off. He sings the first verse and chorus of The Boys of the Old Brigade as his pal drags him out. He sings because he's Irish just like Secret Agent Grace who eavesdrops. The Irish: is there anything they won't stoop to?

# Freddie's bint off?

Freddie and Ada meanwhile get married and this puts Tommoi in an awkward situation. Getting Freddie out of Birmingham was part of the deal with Campballs. Aunt Polly tells the couple to get the fuck to New York with a £200 sweetener. It doesn't appeal. Campballs gets a message to Tommoi – turn in Freddie or Ada gets charged as an accomplice. In a gunpoint set-to Tommoi and Freddie fail to reach accord. Freddie loves Ada and Tommoi loves not being rogered by Campballs.

"This marriage will not stand," he says and nor will he if he takes another buttfucking from the Orangeman.

Tommoi also has to placate his brother Arthur – spazzed out by the war (who isn't?) and feeling left out in the cold because Tommoi keeps making deals behind his back. He's got a point. Tommoi is contrite and points out to his bro that "it's us that has the machine guns now and it's them that's in the mud".

Yeah that's right – reference the war. That always goes down well with the shellshocked.

# Slum deal

It's been a while since someone got killed so Grace braves the slums of Sparkbrook where Citizen Khan will one day make his home. She follows Maguire from earlier and when he makes her from The Garrison it all gets very awkward.

"Proddy bitch! I've seen you. I've seen your face serving in the Garrison." he says, pulling out a pistol. "I am taking you in for interrogation on behalf of the Irish Free State."

Grace doesn't like the sound of that and so she grabs his giant throbbing weapon and eagerly struggles with it. It goes off with a KAPOWWW! and after the gentlest of sighs Maguire is dead. Still he went with a smile on his face. And Grace may be the worst pub singer since Vic Reeves but she's dropping Fenians like Michael Stone. No wonder she's so keen to take up Tommoi's offer of a trip to Cheltenham races – plenty of free Irishmen to murder there.

What she probably doesn't realise is that she's primarily there as bait for Billy Kimber. He likes Grace – who wouldn't? She's a sexually attractive woman even if she has made things a lot worse for Tommoi by offing the IRA man in Sparkbrook. PTSD Danny brings a message from London that the IRA think it's the Peaky Blinders who killed Maguire. This news is as bad as one of the opium fuelled war flashbacks that continue to plague Tom's twilight hours.

## A day at the races

Still, it's off to the races he goes with Grace looking ravishing in a red dress - hey, I hope nobody ravishes her because Grace doesn't get down like that. Tommoi tells her that her new identity is Lady Sarah Duggan of Connemara.

"Don't you mean Cunnymore?" she says, winking.

"No, I mean Connemara. It's a district in the West of Ireland. I thought you were from round there?"

"This cunt's going to take some cracking," thinks Grace as she rapidly accessorises.

Also off to Cheltenham is a newly buoyant Arthur, gathering the Shelby clan to brief them on their mission: Kimber's security have been looking the other way as the Lees duff up the racecourse bookies. The Shelbys will show Billy Kimber how an organisation ruled by violence, fear and intimidation SHOULD behave. By way of demonstration he chops half a Gypsy ear off in the bogs. It's crude but effective.

But it's among the privilege and power of the racecourse ballroom that the real business is being done. Tommoi tells Kimber he wants 5 percent of the take and some legal betting pitches in the North and in return he'll sort out the Lee menace. Kimber leaves the details of the deal to be sorted out by his accountant while he dances with Grace who spends much of the foxtrot avoiding his raddled old boner straining against the fabric of his demob suit.

## A day at the rapes

It all ends in a dinner date round at Billy Kimber's place. Tommoi slips Grace an extra £3 for what will only be 2 hours in his company as Kimber is very confident he can nail her. When his legendary charm doesn't work he resorts to his failsafe rape method™ he picked up from King Edward on The White Queen and all of a sudden that £3 is no longer looking like easy money. But before Kimber can seal his rapey deal Tommoi bursts in and tells him she's a whore with syphilis and that he'd probably best not go there.

It's the most romantic thing anyone has ever done for Grace and she swoons as Tommoi drives her away, both his deal with Kimber and Grace's hymen still intact. It all works out so fabulously like a frigging episode of Entourage.

## Notes and observations

- "My tactics come from my experiences in France. Most of my great lumps of men served in France too, sir." Once again Campballs' non-existent war record comes under scrutiny this time from Sergeant Moss. He is getting badly pwn3d in these exchanges.

- Campballs gives Grace a dressing down for killing the Taig which is a bit rich coming from the only human to have killed as many Irishmen as she. He's mainly worried that her judgement is clouded, since her da' was killed by the 'RA in Armagh but he's quite wrong on that. She did it because she just loves killing Paddies so much.

- "You hear that, boys? The same whistles they used to blow to send us over the top, they now blow to try and break us up." Give Freddie his due – he's really got his post-war class war rhetoric down pat.

- "Men always tell their troubles to a barmaid. What is it you and Freddie are fighting over?" She won't win any prizes for subtlety but Grace is a born grifter.

- To make up for the bullets, bombs and betrayal Tommoi buys Arthur The Garrison which at last puts something resembling a smile on the miserable old Nose's face. Can't help thinking that putting a known substance abuser in charge of a pub is problematic but what the hell?

# Series 1 Episode 4 | My Big Fat Gypsy Wedding

**Travellers' pass**

If there's one thing Tyson Fury, the feature length documentary Knuckle and sundry shite in a bucket Internet callout videos have taught us it's that if you play with gentlemen of Traveller extraction then they will be back at you in force – mob handed and out for blood. And you would think with the Gypsy blood flowing through his veins that Tommoi would know this but so intent is he on expanding the gang's business onto the racecourses he only has tunnel vision for that. The Gypsy Lees burst into the betting shop and fuck it right up leaving a hand grenade in Tommoi's car. It nearly gets young Finn blown to shite and forces Tommoi into a sitdown with Gypsy matriarch Ma Lee where he reveals he's planning to double cross rapey Billy Kimber. He just loves making things complicated for himself this one.

**Spread yourself too, Finn**

In a tale of the totally predictable, Campballs pisses in Tommoi's ear about the stolen guns and Freddie Thorne. They had a deal, 'member? Campballs fears revolution but he fears the wrath of Winston Churchill more. Tommoi washes the salty urine out of his lughole to offer him Stanley Chapman - a bigger Commie fish. Campballs takes the Chapman bait and gives his word that Freddie and Ada will get safe passage out of Birmingham (he's a lying liar lying of course but we'll get to that). Should he get the sack behind this guns bullshit he tells Tommoi "I would do things that would shame the devil". That will include killing Tommoi, his brothers and sister and throwing young Finn to the baby rapists in prison. Seems fair enough - losing your job in this economy? Doesn't bear thinking about.

## Life's a pitch

After last week's epic diplomatic efforts Billy Kimber gives Tommoi a licence for his first legal racecourse betting pitch. It prompts much celebration among the gang and they can't wait to pay back Kimber's generosity by royally fucking him over at the first opportunity. They might want to keep an eye on Secret Agent Grace though as she shamelessly noses around the Blinder's illegal business. Instead, Tommoi rewards her endeavours by making her his classy assistant number bod. He's a bit suspicious of her but he makes out with her in the church to seal the deal anyway. Nicely honey trapped, Grace.

## Never make a ho a housewife

We haven't dealt much with John Shelby, widowered by the war, single father to four kids but now we do he has some wonderful news. He's getting married again! Everyone is delighted for him. Those poor four kids can have a mother again and John can get a ride whenever he wants. Who's the lucky girl, bab? It's Lizzie Stark *record needle scratch*

Whoa, pump your breaks. Skanky Slutbox Stark the former prostitute? This is 1919, sex worker is not the respectable profession it is in 2013 that can get you a book deal and entire career cunting off about how great it is to suck cock for a living. There's quite a stigma about it. And, BTW, FYI, she's not quite as *former* as she makes out, at least that's Tommoi's suspicion and he should know - he was banging her himself for two years. That girl really loves the cock.

Give her that. No really, give her that. She cannae get enough.

Showing the head for family affairs that made his name Tommoi kills two turds with one stone by arranging a marriage between John and Esme, a crazy Gypsy broad from the Lee clan. It will force an alliance between the Blinders and the Lees and stop John moping around after the brass. It turns out she's something of a looker too so everyone has a Big Fat Gypsy Wedding. There's fireworks, dancing, drinking, puking though, implausibly, no fighting.

Ada's so excited she gives birth to a filthy communist cross breed right there and then. Congratulations Freddie – it's a pinko! Regrettably, the coppers spoil the baby shower and drag Freddie off by his cock to be buggered and tortured in Winson Green. Sounds harsh but as recently pointed out all Marxists hate Britain, life and themselves. It's only right.

**Notes and observations**

- "John, Lizzie Stark's never done a day's work vertical." Polly tells him. What, she doesn't do back alley knee tremblers? This girl is destined for a town called Gettaefuck, PDQ.

- See Tommoi and see Freddie – the same side of a different cunt. Both are leaders, both seek a better world for their loved ones. What is a gang if not a union and what a union if not a gang? I don't know but I think we're about to find out.

- Sergeant Moss inadvertently tortures Stanly Chapman to death although to his credit he feels a bit bad about it which is more than you can say for Campballs.

- "Men and their cocks never cease to amaze me," Aunt Polly speaking, we assume, from extensive personal experience.

- "I'm Irish, I can make a million toasts. May you be in heaven a full half hour before the devil knows you're dead." FFS, Grace - could you be more of a minstrel? This is like when Foster and Allen dressed as leprechauns on Top of the Pops.

# Series 1 Episode 5 | Daddy cruel

## A bit of how's your father

As we drop in on the weird world of Shelbyville, Tommoi tends to Danny's grave which is a bit odd given that we know that Danny is no more dead than Tim Dog. Grace manages to get this information out of world's thickest cunt Arthur and she wonders to herself: if Danny's not in that grave then who is? Arthur has quite a busy schedule this week and he begins by taking a trip to an illegal boxing set-to in Small Heath. The nerve of these people setting up their operation without so much as a courtesy call to the Peaky Blinders, never mind paying the appropriate levy. Arthur is all set to shut them down when he hears a familiar voice, sees a familiar face and feels the familiar emotion of annihilating despair. Hi dad!

Yes, it's Arthur Shelby senior (Tommy Flanagan), one-time patriarch of the Shelby clan. Tommoi tells him to do one but Arthur jnr wants to get to know his pappy again. He learns the auld fella is into casinos now and that he just needs a few quid - £500 should cover it - to make he and Junior millionaires. The Shelby Casino and Hotel will have "gents and dames flocking from all corners - New York, Chicago, Boston..." Hang on – isn't that just three corners?

Whatever. Arthur jumps at the chance to make his millions. His dad looks at him like Walter White looks at Walter Junior all "I spawned this?" They then have a bare knuckle boxing match which pops predictably wins. He raises his son's hand in triumph and announces "this is my beloved son with whom I well pleased". Arthur junior shouts "Oi luv you dad!" as they embrace. Jesus Christ he's thick - even for a Brummie.

## "Are you a RepubliCAN or a RepubliCUNT?"

The stink over Grace's sectarian killing of the Sparkbrook Fenian isn't going away. IRA man Malachi Byrne (Tom Vaughan-Lawlor) appears requesting an audience with Tommoi. The dead man was his cousin and he has a proposal for the Blinders: he wants the stolen guns or the Irish Republican Army wipes them out. Tommoi tells them he will hand them over for a price. Sounds like a good deal – everyone's happy.

But of course he's actually setting them up for Campballs - a big fish for the roguish old prod to land. When negotiations in the Garrison go south Grace comes out blasting, killing one of the IRA men before Tommoi caves in Byrne's skull with a slop bucket. It might sound harsh but you know the IRA's record in Birmingham pubs. Between them Tommoi and Grace have now killed more Irishmen than Oliver Cromwell and there's no indication of them stopping any time soon.

## A previous engagement

There's still the thorny issue of Campballs and his weapons fixation. Grace negotiates Tommoi's immunity from his wrath with the location of the guns – Danny Ryan's grave. He gives her his word and he retrieves the guns from the cemetery plot.

So that's Operation Stolen Gun Retrieval done. Campballs passes on the good news to Churchill and Grace resigns. She feels she no longer has the need to avenge her father.

Campballs takes the opportunity to propose marriage and she takes the opportunity to tell him to eat donkey dick until he dies. In a rare moment of insight Campballs realises that Tommoi is behind the brutal friendzoning. Cockblocked by a Peaky Blinder - oh the infamy!

You can guess what's next. Campballs and his men come for Tommoi - so much for that immunity agreement. Tommoi heads back to Grace's and taps that ass like Morse Code. Campballs watches through the window, masturbating furiously. He decides to call off the hunt for the night. He'll bide his time, something he's got plenty of now he's retired, friendless and dateless.

Still, it could be worse. He could be Arthur. In the world's least surprising development pa dukes GTFO with his eldest and thickest son's money. Arthur remonstrates with the punk but only gets manhandled in return.

"If you ever put your hands on me again, I'll cut your fucking throat and spread you on these tracks" his pops assures him. At least that's a statement you can probably believe. It catapults Arthur into a shitpit of despair. As he reaches rock bottom he makes the one correct decision of his life and gets with hanging himself with the quickness. Being the three-flush turd he is, he even fucks that up.

So it's all set up for the gang to get after rapey Billy Kimber in the finale. Go get 'im boys!

**Notes and observations**

- Viewers may recognise Chibs from Sons of Anarchy playing Shelby senior. Tommy Flanagan is steadily cornering the market in melodramatic Celts in gang dramas.

- Then there's Nidge from Love/Hate showing up as the IRA man - Tom Vaughan-Lawlor doing his bit by steadily cornering the market in angry tiny jackeens getting up in everyone's grill.

- As Campballs retrieves the guns from the cemetery plot, Grace sings a deeply meta version of I Am Stretched on Your Grave to Tommoi. It's kind of cute.

- Freddie's looking well battered in prison and Ada's got the right hump with the family. Fortunately we don't particularly care about either of them so that's good enough with us.

- "You should have used a gun" says Tommoi to Arthur after his hanging attempt. He is right of course although we all know he'd probably miss.

# Series 1 Episode 6 | Small Heath, big gun

## Hooers on first

Having been viciously friendzoned by Grace, Paisley Campballs visits the Chinese quarter to get a ride from a Celestial no doubt buying into orientalist notions of their women's inherent submissiveness. God, he's such a racist. Anyway, Ping-Pong love him long time but he cuts up a little rough and she doesn't want a cuddle afterwards. He really is in a state.

It doesn't help matters when Tommoi pops in for a chat. It gives the opportunity for Campballs to monologue on the key similarities between the two like an A-level English literature essay. The fuck that Tommoi doesn't give about that is extensive.

## Bet noire

Brighter climes beckon him, particularly as he will soon be joining the official National Association of Racecourse Bookmakers, taking his crime family legit and fucking up Billy Kimber's men in the process. He's planning all-out war at Worcester Races - the Blinders and the Lees against Kimber and his crew of flunkies. It's always good to have a veteran on the team so they bust Freddie out of custody with the help of a bent guard and PTSD Danny. Ada reconciles with Tommoi and has named her boy Karl after Karl Marx. Things are looking good for the Shelbys.

Not so for Grace who meets with that thick buck Sergeant Moss who hands her a letter from Campballs then calls her an auld hooer. Hey, best not to slut shame Grace, fatty. She's killed more Irishmen than the potato blight. In the letter Campballs drizzles on about the sprained vagina he suffered as a result of her rejection of his marriage proposal. Worse is to follow as he drops her right in it by tipping the Kimbers off to Tommoi's doublecross. They are heading up the Stratford Road to snuff the Peaky Blinders out. Tommoi quietly swallows something hard and jagged – betrayed by a black velvet band!

Polly visits Grace to badmouth her and Grace is appalled – that's the worst Birmingham accent she's ever heard.

"Seriously, where the fuck are you supposed to be from?" she asks "That doesn't even sound European."

Polly isn't waylaid by her vocal critique though and gives her a choice: leave or die. Grace takes a moment before deciding that leaving is probably the better of those two options.

## Life in the blast lane

Back in Garrison Lane, the Blinders are outnumbered 3-to-1. The Kimber men approach. John and Freddie bring out the remaining British machine gun and it's like prohibition America. As the crews face-off against each other with guns drawn Ada rolls up and gives a really shit junior debating society speech about boys and their guns making widows and it has an immediate impact. Kimber starts blasting just to drown out her noise. Ada's speechifying has much the same effect as Grace's singing. She makes men cry though rarely for the reason she intends.

The first slug twats Tommoi in the shoulder, the second hits Danny who's dead for real this time. But Tommoi Shelby didn't wade through the shit and blood of the Somme to go out like that. He expertly pops a bullet in Kimber's noggin and he JFK's his brains all over the cobbles.

"Kimber and me fought this battle one on one. It's over." Tommoi tells Kimber's men. "Go home to your families."

They are inclined to agree, meekly dragging their fallen king off and getting home for Match of the Day. I hope no one was getting paid by the hour. McGregor-Aldo lasted longer.

**Biting the bullet**

So after a bit of battleground surgery to remove the bullet all that's left is for Tommoi to toss a coin to decide what to do about Grace. The result is tails he dumps her saying that running off to America like a little bitch is not how he gets down. And thus does the century's greatest love affair end landing very firmly on the wrong side of the whimper-bang spectrum.

But that is because they are two sexually attractive adults who will both be boning other people within 24 hours. For the really sensational relationship endings you need to look to the incel community. And who better to represent that than Campballs? He turns up on the railway platform just as Grace is about to board the 11.45 to Anywhere But His General Trouser Area and in a fit of blue balls-fuelled rage at her deception, rejection and inception he pulls out a Glock 9mm out of his purse. A bang is heard but we don't actually see who gets shot. Remember, we do know that Grace likes to pack heat and I'm not just talking about her fanny.

If he has killed her then millions of Irishmen around the world will breathe a sigh of relief as this self-hating genocidal maniac is finally put to bed. As a Brucie Bonus we never have to hear that skank sing again.

I do love a happy ending.

## Notes and observations

- "God says he don't deal with Small Heath." Jeremiah briefly going off-message from the good book for the Garrison Lane rumble.

- "We hate people and they in turn hate us". That may well be true Campballs but I think the key difference is Tommoi doesn't have to pay for pussy, you raddled old fuck.

- "Some things never change. Eh, sir?" Sergeant Moss telling Campballs that essentially it was all for nothing. He's got a real smart mouth on him when he's in the mood.

- Polly opens up to Ada about her two children Sally and Michael who were taken away from her. It was a different age where you could lose custody of your spawn just for being a filthy criminal.

- Shelby Brothers Limited is now the third largest legal racetrack betting concern in the country. Tommoi's quest to legitimise the Shelby family continues apace. Truly, he is the Michael Corleone of Birmingham. And I'm pretty certain he turned out just *fine*.

# Series 2 Episode 1 | Birmingham, are you listening?

## Coup de Grace

Now that the last gangster has been run out of Small Heath with Peeturd Pannu's departure how about we head back to 1920s Birmingham and reunite with the Peakoi Bloinders? Hurrah! As PJ Harvey's To Bring You My Love blares we learn it was Secret Agent Grace shooting Campballs the Taig Killer in the first series finale and not the other way around. I suppose in the end she just couldn't stop killing Irishmen even if they incorrectly self-identified as British. Tommoi would be so proud. We fast forward to two years later. Two broads leave prams outside the Garrison and blow it to shit. Birmingham is known for its pub bombings and while this is not one of the more spectacular ones it's enough to get the attention. The Irish – is there anything they won't explode?

That despicable red Freddie Thorne is well out of this life. He's dead like a cunt from influenza and Tommoi takes the opportunity of his funeral to try to persuade Ada to come home. He plans an expansion of his criminal empire into Londung and that could make things tricky for a single mother communist Shelby girl. Ada laughs in the face of danger though and she tells him to smoke some cock for kicks. "Woi wanna boi together!" she mocks as she struts off back to the Pit. No need for that, bab.

## Lowering the bar

Tommoi can't afford to dwell on this vicious sibling abuse as he has the bombed pub fallout to deal with. He visits the Black Lion, an Irish bar in Digbeth. "Yow blew up moii pub" he tells them through an interpreter in a disgraceful act of racial profiling. He's right of course but that doesn't make it any better. The simple fact is you can't put an Irishman inside a Birmingham pub without him trying to destroy it. It's as ingrained into their culture as bacon and cabbage, paedophile priests and shitty non-stories in their newspapers about members of U2.

Irene O'Donnell is the Fenian he's currently addressing. Her male companion puts a gun to his head.

"Well if you're going to put a gun to my head..." he says.

"Shut your fucking Gypsy mouth and listen to your instructions" says Irene. Whoa, come on Irene. No need to resort to ethnic slurs you spud chomping fuck.

In any event, it winds up with Tommoi plugging some Mick called Eamonn Duggan at the steelworks. Labour relations were less bogged down in red tape in those simpler happier times.

Speaking of Mick killers, Inspector Campballs is back on the scene, walking with a stick now but still ethnically cleansing the Irish as head of the Irish Desk, some secret intelligence agency or other. He persuades Winston Churchill to let him have another crack at Birmingham. He has unfinished business there.

## Capital crimes

But for now it's down to London Tommoi, Arthur and John go. There's a gang war between the Italians led by Darby Sabini and the Jews led by Alfie Solomons and the Blinders need to pick a side. Tommoi chooses the Chosen People and to announce his decision he rolls up at Sabini's jazz club. Honestly, a telegram would have done. He's such a drama queen.

Sabini doesn't appreciate the gesture and it escalates rather quickly into a big bar fight. Despite being outnumbered 39 to 1 and the Italians having machine guns, flamethrowers and mustard gas it's the Shelby brothers who emerge triumphant. It's the kind of futile yet dramatic gesture certain to send shockwaves through the criminal underworld.

Yeah, there are waves alright and upon his return to Brum Tommoi gets swamped by one. He is beaten like a Chris Brown groupie by Sabini and his flunkies for about an hour, the crew of shortarse greaseballs taking it in turns to wail on him. Sabini thoughtfully throws in some complementary pre-NHS dental work that makes him look like Shane McGowan.

"You shouldn't have" says Tommoi, spitting blood and teeth "No really, you shouldn't have".

Just as he's about to get killed dead in the head who should come and save him but Inspector Campballs. He's not done with Tommoi yet and neither are we. Bloody hell!

## Strike a crappy medium

Elsewhere, Polly is getting shitty dreams about her shitty daughter she lost through being a shitty parent all those years ago. In the dreams her daughter tells her she's all dead and shit and so Polly goes to a shitty medium. We don't actually see the reading proper but Pol runs out screaming "NO! NO! NOOOOOOO!" which either means she let it slip about Valentino dying in a few years or her daughter's dead like a little bitch. Or, you know, mediums are worthless psychic Tampax for the weak and desperate. Whichever you prefer.

**Notes and observations**

- Down in Londung, Ada gets herself abducted. She'll be getting bummed senseless if I know Italians. Deary me.

- My God this show loves killing the Irish. The Irish diaspora in 1919 numbered roughly 9 million. After Peaky Blinders' first series it was 112. Just saying.

- Winston Churchill is now played by Richard McCabe not Andy Nyman as before. Churchill joins the TV actor replacement Hall of Fame along with Spartacus, Ann Veal, Lucy Robinson and Marilyn Munster.

- "Karl's with his cousins. I caught 'em trying to pinch flowers off a grave." Aunt Polly confirming that the garbage Shelby DNA has consigned another generation to criminality.

- Exciting times ahead for Lizzie Stark as she transitions from sucking cock for a living into secretarial work for a criminal conspiracy. Tommoi's recruitment policy continues to astound.

# Series 2 Episode 2 | Coke is it!

**Injury time**

TV in general is a bit too rapey these days so it's a pleasant surprise when a Peakoi Bloinder interrupts the violation of Ada. We can easily do without that. Meanwhile over in the Revenge Beating Injuries ward in Selly Oak Hospital, Tommoi gets a visit from Campballs the Taig Killer. They reminisce over Secret Agent Grace – married now in New York, presumably not to a music fan.

"That was some sweet Mick pussy." says Tommoi.

"I'll take your word for it." says Campballs sadly. He's such an incel bag of shit. The last trim he saw was his mother's as he exited it.

But he has not come here to be reminded that he will die a virgin. He's come to tell Tommoi that he knows it was he who killed Eamonn Duggan and that he can therefore blackmail him to do like whatever he wants.

"You belong to me," he whispers. Homoerotic tension rises.

The conversation prompts Tommoi into action. Despite having fatal brain damage, seven crushed vertebrae, a shattered pelvis, compound fracture of the femur, dislocated pubic bone, broken sternum and sprained vagina he discharges himself from hospital. He can't think about convalescence when there are deals to be done.

## The Gentile touch

And like so many sons of Birmingham before him, he's off down to London on the barge, swigging rub alcohol, Bovril and PG Tips.

"Orroight!" he shouts at the first Londoners he sees before collapsing face first into a coma. And he's the brains of the family.

He meets up with Alfie Solomons (Tom Hardy), King of the Jews. He's not the *real* King of the Jews of course as they crucified him. Still, Alfie has quite a few rackets going operating from his bakery. He doesn't see an alliance with the Blinders as a kosher move, particularly when it was Tom who put one in Billy Kimber's dome. For the 49th time this series Tommoi has a gun to his head and it's just possible it's starting to lose its impact. Despite his aggression, Solomons listens. He is intrigued by this handsome gypo. He probably wants to fuck him just like everyone else.

## Cocaine's a hell of a drug

Back at home, world's thickest cunt Arthur is still having Grant Mitchell style Falklands flashbacks and in the throes of one he beats a nine-year-old boy to death. Everyone agrees it was a fair fight though and the kid almost certainly had it coming.

Still, it's a warning sign that Arthur may kill a person somebody actually gives a shit about and with the Garrison reopening imminent the Shelbys need their boy in top form. Finn's solution is to get Arthur hooked on coke which is *exactly* what a homicidal maniac needs. The bash at the Garrison is a huge success and even that miserable old sow Polly gets some ass. There's a whole lot of fucking going on in fact but even with a roomful of hookers Tommoi can't orgy Grace out of his mind. That was some tidy Irish pumpum right enough.

## Dramatic licence

And despite what many think Tommoi is not just about psychotic acts of violence. He can commit atrocities with the written word as well. He dictates a letter to Winston Churchill through his new secretary Lizzie Stark, who takes the cock out of her mouth just long enough to scribble it down in elementary shorthand.

The broad gist is that Tommoi fought like a real G at Verdun and the Somme, has copped more medals than Michael Phelps and is the greatest soldier the world has ever seen. The very least Winnie can do is grant him an Empire export licence for his criminal enterprise?

"Come on old boy – soldier to soldier. Whaddyasay??

Yore pal, Thomas Shelby.
Military Medal, DCM Distinguished Conduct Medal and proud Bluenose. KRO. SOTV."

Remarkably, it does the trick. Despite Campballs' reservations that Tommoi is a "murdering cut-throat mongrel gangster" Churchill agrees to bung an export licence Tommoi's way at least until he carries out an assassination for them and then they can kill him and yoink the licence away Top Cat style. Campballs is good with that.

## Keeping mum

Ultimately, though Tommoi is really all about family. He vows to Polly that he will track down her remaining spawn and true to his word he turns up at the doorstep of a perfectly happy household in the sticks where Polly's son Michael has an idyllic, healthy and sane upbringing. And it's clearly driving him mad. Despite his fake mom's protestations he takes Tommoi's card. A new life of danger, sluts and impenetrable accents awaits.

As we finish, Michael turns up as Polly arrives at Casa Shelby. She reeks of sex, gin and is as pissed as a twat and that's the best way to be when viewing this spectacularly dull subplot.

## Notes and observations

- The Blinder who stopped Ada's rape might reasonably anticipate a thank-you, perhaps even the criminal underworld's equivalent of a commendation. No good deed goes unpunished though and instead he gets a kick in the balls for his trouble. Don't mention it Ada! Oh, you didn't.

- Being a Shelby woman isn't all bad though. Thanks to the new policy of putting property in family members' names Ada cops an eight-bedroom house in Primrose Hill and Polly lands swanky digs in Bournville. Too bad for her that the gaff is on Quaker land where no pubs or off-licences are allowed.

- "I've read very bad, bad, bad things about you Birmingham people." Alfie Solomons just can't put down Ozzy Osbourne's autobiography.

- Now that Campballs knows that Moss is on the Blinders payroll he has him playing double agent and you can't help thinking the unfortunate sergeant is going to find that just terribly confusing.

- It's becoming increasingly clear that the dude who plays Sabini, Noah Taylor, can't act a lick. If he gets any hammier then Campballs will have him in a sandwich with pickle.

# Series 2 Episode 3 | Digbeth slid

**Bother from another mother**

The great thing about being a Peaky Blinder on the TV show Peaky Blinders is that everybody knows you're a Peaky Blinder. And they just can't *wait* to tell you about the bang-up job you're doing. Take the mother of that smart mouthed kid Arthur slapped to death, who comes down to the Garrison to have words with him.

"I'm not a cleaner" she says pulling out an Uzi "But I've come to CLEANER WAY SOME DIRT!"

"Sick burn," says Arthur "Been working on that one long?"

"You killed my son, you Peaky bastard! You beat him and beat him and beat him." she reminds us in case we popped out during the 'previously on'.

In a rare moment of insight he tells her that the trouble is in his shit head. "DO IT!" he commands in that way that only people on TV do. She'd happily comply with the request but she's shaking like Judy Finnigan after her debut on Loose Women. She leaves without getting her round in but Arthur survives so he should probably chalk that one up as a win.

## Zionist agenda

In an attempt to make the Blinders' dicey Birmingham accents sound convincing, Tommoi recruits old wartime comrade Billy Kitchen - a filthy ignorant yam-yam with an even more pish Black Country accent. Billy will be heading up the platoon of Dingles and Boggies Tommoi sends down to Camden to work in Alfie Solomons' rum running operation.

"The first rule of Shite Club is you do not talk about Shite Club." Alfie tells them "The second rule is you can't bang Jewish broads. Jewish men are fine though. We all get lonely."

That all seems fair enough and after an unprovoked savage act of violence against one of the noobs, Alfie wanders off to do some synagogueing or whatever it is they do. I don't think anyone ever *really* knows, you know? It's part of the reason why they run everything.

## Doing it for the Kids

Say what you like about the Blinders but they do a lot of good work in the community, providing work for many unfortunates. Some local dope calling himself the Digbeth Kid does a week in Winson Green clink for the crew. It's a piece of piss for a £5 payday - shelter, one square meal a day and PJ Harvey piped through the stereo.

Unfortunately for the boy Sabini wants to make a point and the only way to do it apparently is by murdering a completely useless piece of shit with a gang service record lasting less than 24 hours. A knife to the guts and the Digbeth Kid is wormfood. As useless a turd as he was you can't have cockney greaseballs murdering Blinders in their hometown prison so Tommoi sets the revenge plan in motion. He also sets up the Digbeth Kid Memorial Fund for Illiterate Bradford Street Tramps. His death was not in vain in stark contrast to his life.

## Getting killy for the filly

That Sabini is being a right pain in the arse and to fast-track the plan to move on his racetracks Tommoi eyes up a racehorse. The grey filly will set him back 1000 guineas but she'll be a great Trojan horse to get the gang into the Epsom Derby owners enclosure so it's off to auction they go. And wouldn't you know it when they get there Tommoi gets cuntstruck by a posh bird again. This time it's May Fitz-Carleton (Charlotte Riley) who doubles his outlay by bidding against him for the grey. She buttonholes him afterwards and wonders what he does.

"I do bad things but you already knew that."

She certainly fucking hopes so. May tells him to hit her up on WhatsApp and once again Tommoi is about to fall for the wrong dame.

"Rich women these days – all they want is working class cock" says Arthur callously stealing the line that I would have written.

Fucking Arthur. The dimwit PTSD calamity is put to good use however when Brother Sabini and his men make an assassination attempt on Tommoi and Arthur gives him an almighty hiding followed by a lovebite. It's the little touches that count.

"Will no one rid me of this turbulent wop?" cries Tommoi.

Give it a couple of weeks, son. I have a feeling he'll get his.

## Notes and observations

- You have to hand it to Tommoi. If there's a pretty, unobtainable and almost certainly lethal female around, he's on that skank like Jimmy Savile on your granny's mortuary slab.

- "I recommend the Daily Mail, it will broaden your mind." Well, there's a first time for everything Campballs.

- "No! Fucking no!" Polly upon hearing Michael wants to get involved with the family business. I think that's a no? She relents when she realises that the trash Shelby DNA in his cells will always come through no matter how many posh boy affectations he has. Michael's on board.

- The Irish problem is active on the streets of Birmingham with Micks killing each other with reckless abandon. They must feel confident in their numbers now that Grace has taken her genocidal campaign across the Atlantic.

- Campballs doesn't take it well when Tommoi reveals the coppers deliberately stuck him in a knocking shop. He just can't handle the bantz.

# Series 2 Episode 4 | Jew model Army

## Poor Paddy

A dreaded bummy day so we'll meet you at the cemetery gates. Tommoi rolls up to the Digbeth Kid's funeral to get slapped by a long line of Deritend residents like the hysterical woman in Airplane. It's fun for a while getting smacked about like Lindsey Buckingham's live-in lover but in the end he bungs them a few quid to stop. There's always something and the next always something is a meeting with Campballs and those two pro-Treaty Micks who blew up the Garrison. It looks like they've been in cahoots forever - and nobody thought to tell Tommoi. There's another anti-Treaty chump they want iced and so happy were they with his last murder, they've decide to hire him again. Who says you can't trust Gypsy labour?

Tommoi has a few misgivings about the gig though. He privately tells Campballs that the smart mouthed Mick Donal Henry is a spy for the Irregulars, reporting back to his Guinness and rabbit stewing brethren. Tommoi will do the murder if they kill Henry. Well, if it means more dead Irishmen then Campballs is definitely down with that.

## This snorting life

Down in Camden Town, Arthur leads an army of Jews into the Italian Gomorrah of Sabini's jazz club. In a terrifying display of Jew rage they force many of the punters into loans with unfavourable repayment rates, replace the calzone with chicken soup & matzah balls and write "WE DID THIS" on the idolatrous crucifix hanging over the stage. Talk about a liberty.

They announce that the club is under new management and incredibly Arthur doesn't kill a child in the process. And you know what that means: coke and hookers orgy! Arthur is still getting high on his own supply and Tommoi takes him to task for his disgraceful habit. If he doesn't buck up and get clean he'll hand the London operation over to John. Arthur assures him that he can keep off the Tokyo but we all know perfectly well he will be doing more gak than peak Stevie Nicks for the remainder of the series.

## Daniel Amokachi

But hey what about Michael son of Polly and proud holder of a City and Guilds certificate? Well it's his 18th birthday and to celebrate he takes his black best friend Chalky to the Marquis of Lorne for a celebration drink. Wouldn't you know it though their evening is ruined by a racist Liverpudlian who takes umbrage at having to share the same bar as a person of colour. Slavery has yet to be abolished in Liverpool and it will be 70 years before Everton sign a black player so this was really to be expected. Some fisticuffs ensue and some harsh words are exchanged. There's no major damage done though until Arthur hears about the ruckus and burns the place to the ground with the landlord in it.

## Mounting the mare

Back in the world of horse racing May Fitz-Carleton takes Tommoi's filly away to train. He calls the nag Grace's Secret and he really wants to let that one go. Grace is happily married in America and she certainly WON'T be coming back any time soon.

As if to confirm this he pays May a visit at her palace plonked in the middle of her 50 billion acre estate. She tells him she's as lonely as a bastard in her gigantic castle. "Like a fucking lighthouse keeper" she says.

They bond over Grace's Secret and he totally bones her. The toff not the horse – unless things took a dark turn during the night.

## Zion flamer

Things are definitely taking a dark turn in That London as Sabini and Alfie Solomons meet to see who can put in the most scenery chewing performance of a loose cannon gang boss. Sabini wins of course. Sabini always wins. It seems that their quarrel stems from Alfie taking offence at Sabini's harmless anti-Semitic banter.

"All the fucking time - dirty fucking Jews, dirty Kikes, dirty dustbin lids..."

"A joke's a joke, Alfie" says Sabini.

"Bagel dog, hook nose, Bible shortener, Heebie, Christ killer..."

"Come on mate – we go back years."

"Cliptip, four by two, German candle, Himey, Shylock, Jewbacca, Jewgaboo..."

"Fuck's sake – I don't even know half of those."

"Lampshade, penny chaser, sausage dodger, snipcock, Yahoodi - you get my point?"

He kind of does. They reach an accord to squash their beef and run the Blinders' Yam-Yam platoon out of town. This could certainly impact on Tommoi's new racket - exporting single malt Scotch to prohibition quenched Canada. Jews, man. You just can't leave them alone for a minute.

Even more dangerous for Tommoi is the package that's just arrived at the Ritz Londung. It's Secret Agent Grace! And she's accompanied by her American husbland. We'll assume she's not there for a singing gig. Tommoi crank calls her room pretending to be *Dick Gozinya*. Thank God he's kept his dignity.

**Notes and observations**

- "You want to fuck me, Mrs Carleton? Perhaps because I would represent something to you?" Quick note for incels: this only works for the sexually attractive. Even with the psychoanalysis rider this talk will get you nothing but a smack in the chops.

- So now Michael is the new Peaky Blinders accountant – the man who will steer the ship from the rocky outcrops of criminality into the calm waters of legitimacy. Well, that's the theory. I'm not sure if employing this class tourist is going to help achieve Tommoi's dream.

- It's good that Tommoi's still a realist then. He sets up a trust fund for Ada and John's kids so that in the event of him buying the farm they get a nice lump sum. If that's not motivation to finally kill him I don't know what is.

- Field Marshal Henry Russell is Tommoi's target for assassination. Exactly why he's an enemy of the Crown is unclear but security around the bozo is crazy. This is no dumb Mick staggering home pissed from the pub. Nothing could ever be simple.

- The insurance policy is already in place. Tommoi tells Campballs that should he mysteriously die during or after the assassination then the instructions are to make Campbell's Soup of the gobby gimp. You might have thought that Campballs would welcome death but while there are still Irishmen alive to be killed he's seeing this one out for the duration.

# Series 2 Episode 5 | Yahweh or the highway

**The wrong Good Friday**

Now that Arthur's been down in the capital for a few months, it's time for Alfie to explain to him the origins of the Jewish festival Passover. "Well see me old mucker - Moses was one of your own. Not like your Pharaoh oppressing and enslaving and whatnot. Moody cunt. So your old Yahweh killed all of your Egyptians' firstborns. You understand, me old china?"

"I don't," admits Arthur "But my seemingly infinite stupidity coupled with my pathetic need for a father figure has allowed me to let my guard down and see this monologuing faggotry as a friendly chat rather than the Very Bad Thing it clearly is."

"You not wrong there, pal..." says Alfie and with that Billy Kitchen the Dingle gets a bullet in the head. A triumphant Sabini walks in as Arthur fumes impotently.

"Oh yeah by the way. That Jesus geezer?" whispers Alfie "We done him too."

"Noooooooooooooooooo!" screams Arthur. He's so sad. Jews, man. Again.

So after clubbing him unconscious, he and Sabini frame Arthur for the Dingle's murder with the help of some friendly coppers. The Constabulary are busy in Birmingham too running up in Polly's crib and arresting Michael for pub arson – the *worst kind* of arson. It has the whiff of a set up about it but it's possible it has something to do with the Marquis of Lorne being torched. Polly doesn't take it well. When does she take anything well? Everything is falling apart and all anyone wants to know is where's Tommoi?

**Polly - wanna smack her?**

As it turns out he's running up May Fitz-Nicely's skirts but when he hears about the mayhem at home, he's back up the M1 faster than a girlfriend of Oscar Pistorius who says "it's only me, Stumpy" after shutting the toilet door. An angry confrontation with Campballs follows. He admits that he is behind Michael's arrest. It is all to assure Tommoi's focus on the upcoming assassination. A bit of overkill there. You don't think text alerts could have done the trick?

Ah but then Campballs wouldn't be alone in a room with Polly, watching her beg for clemency for her boy. As luck would have it Campballs has a release form for Michael on his desk and all he has to do is sign it. But there's a catch. The pricetag is Polly's 48-year-old foof. Ruh-roh!

He's selling himself a bit short there. Let's be honest at its absolute prime Polly's quim would fetch tuppence tops and he's perverting the course of justice here. Anyway he gets a quick ride for his trouble and pops her one in the jaw - not for any sexual reason, just because Polly is very annoying.

As Michael is released, he tells Polly that the prison officers all had a big laugh at her giving up the nappy dugout for his freedom. He's not happy about that and nor is she. I bet Campballs isn't too chuffed either. It's a shitty deal all round.

## Grace under firewater

It all makes you wonder what Campballs would give up to bang Secret Agent Grace, who pays a visit to Tommoi. It's a tense reconciliation between the pair but after 19 shots of whiskey and reminiscing about all the Irishmen they've killed they start to loosen up. Tommoi takes her to meet Charlie Chaplin who he knows through the secret underground Gypsy network that has been running Hollywood for decades. Grace melts in the face of all the glamour. She's in the bag. And Tommoi can't wait to phone and tell Campballs.

"I'm totally about to bang Grace," he says "What do you think about that you crippled scenery chewing Prod?"

"I'm incredibly lonely" says Campballs tearfully and it's probably for the best that Tommoi had already hung up at that point.

And he *totally* bangs Grace again. In the nuddy and everything - she even takes her bra off. She's a decent enough ride, right enough, but her postcoital pillow talk needs some work.

"I'm having me giblets seen to." she tells him "Or whatever the 1920s equivalent of IVF is."

"What am I then?" he asks "Some kind of spunk donor?"

It certainly looks that way. There is every chance there will soon be another addition to the Shelby clan, which is *exactly* what the world needs.

But before all that is the assassination of Field Marshal Russell which Tommoi now informs Campballs will happen at the Derby. What with that, preparing Grace's Secret for the big race and taking over Sabini's bookmakers it looks like being a busy day.

## Notes and observations

- "I have a great curiosity. Like a magpie sees something, something shining in the mud. Oh, he has no need for the silver, but he takes it anyway." In case you were wondering, yes that is Polly's vagina Campballs is referring to.

- "To remind meself what I'd be if I wasn't who I am." Tommoi's answer to the not unreasonable question "why are you shovelling shit you handsome bastard?"

- Campballs seems to get some weird masochistic thrill from Tommoi banging Grace. It would make a lot of sense if he had a cucking fetish like Norman "Cuck" Cook.

- "You think your people are ruthless? Try mine." May dropping truth bombs on Tommoi from the lofty perch of the English aristocracy.

- "Imagine riding away, Thomas. Living the real life, you know? Your Gypsy half is the stronger. You just want to ride away. France is the new place for us, they say." Fascinating pitch from Esme, exhorting Tommoi to embrace his Gypsy roots. As for France as the promised land for travelling folk - well you can't be right about everything.

# Series 2 Episode 6 | Red hand gang

## I was looking for a rhyme for the New York Times

Tommoi Shelby will be the first to admit that he's not much of a letter writer. Scrawling "Oi'm gonna kill yow" on a chitty then stapling it to the forehead of a debtor is about his limit. And yet we find him writing a letturd to the Editor of the New York Times, the gist of which is that if he's dead when the editor receives it it's all Campballs' fault. How exactly the New York Times editor is expected to tell Tommoi's shitty letter from all the other letters from lunatics newspaper editors receive is not made clear. The important thing is that Tommoi thinks it matters and with his big day at the races coming up that's all that matters.

Before all that though he takes a trip with Gay James for an outing to Alfie Solomons'. For the 350,000th time this series Tommoi gets a gun pointed at his head and people really need to start learning that this changes nothing for him. Kill the cunt or don't but you may as well be making pistol fingers at him as pressing a barrel to his temple. After some World War I ammunition fuelled brinksmanship he negotiates a 35% cut for Solomons of their exports dealings and the Gypsy-Jew alliance is back on.

# Derby and blown

And so with a freshly released Arthur it's off to the Derby they all go. May Fitz-Nicely's looking predictably smoking yet doomed but Secret Agent Grace messes with her hustle, turning up unannounced like a proper cockblock. As predicted, she's pregnant with Tommoi's babby in record time. His fecundity is legendary, his sperm are legion and his balls are magic.

"I love you not him," she tells him as May makes the blowjob gesture at her behind his back. Later the two ladies have a long discussion over the merits of Tommoi's cock and the benefits and perils of their membership of the international sisterhood of sexually attractive women. You can tell they are both thinking "threesome" but are too proud to say it.

Tommoi's too busy to get into that conversation as he's got a Field Marshal to fuck up. Using Lizzie as a honeypot to isolate Russell in one of the many Fuck Stalls owners enclosures routinely have installed, Tommoi ends his life with a bullet through the brain after a titanic struggle that leaves Tommoi with an eye jammie and Lizzie with a bruised fanny. She's hella pissed at Tommoi for leaving her with her arse quite literally hanging out and encourages her short lived fiancé John to take the road less travelled away from his life of crime, riches and hot Gypsy wife. The sales pitch needs a bit of work but her heart's in the right place.

Fortunately, things go more smoothly on the track with the Blinders bum rushing Sabini's bookmaking pitches and burning their licences. Tommoi stops off at the bar to rub Campballs' nose in it about Grace again. You notice he's never too busy to do that? Campballs doesn't have to suffer the insolence much longer though as Polly ices him in a Fuck

Stall disguised as a phone box. "Ring, ring motherfucker" she said as he slumps to the ground as dead as a Geldof locked in a room with a Geldof parent.

**Churchill insurance? Oh yes.**

So it's a win-win win-WIN for Tommoi who is starting to feel that things are finally going his way. The feeling quickly dissipates when the three UVF men Campballs set up to kill him abduct him and bring him to a big empty field with a freshly dug grave with his name on it. So it all ends here.

"So fucking close!" he wails.

He wrangles a last fag out of them before settling down to enjoy the firing squad.

It turns out to be a lot more fun than he had anticipated. Just as he's about to get plugged UVF man #3 puts one each in the dome of his comrades. He informs Tommoi that Winston Churchill will be in touch with a job for him and if he wouldn't mind running along so he can bury the two Ulstermen that would be splendid. Bloody Churchill, eh?

Tommoi howls with grief – he thought he'd got away with it. He'll have to pay child support now. And even worse is facing him when he gets back. Michael is ignoring every piece of good commonsense advice out there and choosing Birmingham over London. He's starting to wish that fake UVF man had done him instead.

Nonetheless, he does reveal that he's planning on getting married. Possibly to a girl. What's he like?

## Notes and observations

- We learn from Tommoi that Field Marshal Russell has a past as a Black and Tan commander who "committed many atrocities". So fuck that guy basically.

- Charles Ransom Miller who Tommoi writes to explaining the Campballs conspiracy was editor of the New York Times for 40 years. He once referred to the European papers as "the reptile press that crawls on its belly every day to the foreign office of the government officials and ministers to know what it may say or shall say". Sounds like Tommoi would have got a sympathetic audience had the letter ever been sent.

- "He's like one of those anarchists that blew up Wall Street." Tommoi bigging up Gay James a bit here but the anarchists he refers to are real. They killed 30 and were never apprehended.

- Polly dumps a load of cash on Michael and orders him to a new life in London. Perhaps she hasn't heard that London is now crawling with Peaky Blinders?

- "Today, it'll be me dead, or you, but whoever it is, is gonna wake up in hell tomorrow." Tommoi with a stinging rebuke to Campballs' "certainty of salvation" horseshit.

# Series 3 Episode 1 | White power

## Wedding day blues

It is now 1924, two years since Tommoi faced the Loyalist death squad and lived. Britain has its first Labour Prime Minister, Harold Abrahams brings back the 100m gold medal from the Paris Olympics and Mount Everest delivers a brutal turding to George Mallory. And Tommoi? He's attending a wedding – his own as it happens. Church bells ring out as the illiterate chav clan Shelby try and figure out which way up they should be holding the hymn books. Benjamin Zephaniah is the Minister and the mystery bride is brought by a cavalryman, watched by a couple dozen of his regimental fellows in the pews. It's Secret Agent Grace! But she is Secret Agent Grace no longer. Say "Orroight, bab?" to Mrs Thomas Shelby.

The do is quite something. Tommoi, Grace and their infant son Charles live in Warwickshire in Shelby Palace – 3,957 rooms, 14 million acres of land and a Downton Abbey staff. Tommoi lives like landed gentry but he still has that dangerous edge that makes him the most unpredictable gypsy since Tyson Fury.

## Can you stop the cavalry?

But just like a Sicilian Godfather on his daughter's wedding day Tommoi has to put his affairs in order. Gathering his generals in the kitchen he acknowledges that the presence of the cavalry is something of an affront to his boys. Apparently something about waiting two weeks in the mud for them during the war. Honestly, the slightest thing with these people. Nonetheless, as they are Grace's family, he has a few ground rules for the day

"No cocaine. No sport. No telling fortunes. No racing. No fucking sucking petrol out of their fucking cars."

Well, why even have a wedding if you can't do any of that?

**Rights for Whites**

There are murmurs of the new Russian business interests Tommoi has been recently developing. He talks with Russian refugee Anton Kaledin. He tells him that a Duke's niece will be dropping off the $10,000 which we assume is not a donation to Tommoi's Shelby Foundation charity. We gather it is for a factory break-in though the nature is as yet unclear. Fortunately for the viewer we have Secret Agent Grace on the case and she had already boned the truth out of Tommoi as she explains to Polly.

"Royalist Russians buying weapons to fight the Bolsheviks in Georgia. A lost cause, Tommoi says. Churchill is the go-between but it's against government policy so everything must be kept a secret."

Right, gotcha - the Whites and the Reds. We did know Churchill had a job offer for Tom. The thing is that Tom has promised Grace that the Shelby family will be going legit. The foundation, the racetracks, car sales, shooting pheasants and church fetes – that is their future. Charles will never know the power afforded the man grasping the cold steel of a revolver.

You know who does though? Duchess Tatiana Petrovna (Gaite Jansen), aforementioned Duke's niece who arrives packing a firearm, icy glare and killer bod. She also has the $10,000 to be given to Kaledin but there seems to be a problem with that guy. He gave the wrong code name and old Churchill is a bit of a stickler for those. If some wiseass Bolshevik spy from the Soviet embassy infiltrates their pro-White caper then Project Mother Russia is dead in the water along with 13 million 17-year-olds in the world war that will follow. So Kaledin has got to go.

With his newfound (relative) sobriety and semi-attractive Christian wife, Arthur is finding the prospect of killing Kaledin a bit of a bind. Tommoi explains to his simpleton sibling that now that they are employed by the Her Majesty's Government they really have no choice. Plus, it's life changing money.

"Now, we've never earned money like this. Never. We'll use it to buy the wharf at Boston docks. That's why I've asked for dollars."

That's the master plan. So Arthur goes ahead and kills the chump, getting a chunk bitten out of his finger in the process. He looks sickened by the entire ugly business and I'm not talking about his face.

**Minus one plus one**

It wouldn't be a Shelby wedding without some honour violence. That ridiculous old ride Lizzie Stark complains bitterly that her greaseball borefriend Angel got his restaurant firebombed the night before – a clear ploy to keep him from accompanying her to the wedding. Homeboy is mobbed up with the Wop Mafia and the Shelby boys aren't looking to make any gangster alliances just yet. Steer clear of the guido is the clear message.

**Paint me like one of your attractive girls**

If you're anything like me then the fate of Polly is of less consequence than the prospect of a Brother Beyond reunion. Nonetheless, she's still breathing and there is nothing you, I or Bobby "Boogaloo" Watts can do about it. Enigmatic portrait artist Ruben Oliver takes a shine to her at the wedding. The crackle between them is obvious and it's not just the chafing of Polly's ancient labia.

That night he channels the 13th Duke of Wybourne and knocks on her bedroom door with a bottle of champers and 3/5ths of an erection, the closest he's got to full tumescence in decades. Being the classy lady she isn't though Polly demurs. It's too bad as well because she could really do with the ride. She steals his champagne, tells him to GTFO, dusts the cobwebs off her flaps and silently faps herself to sleep. It's the best night she's had in years.

**Notes and observations**

- This week's soundtrack features Nick Cave and the Bad Seeds - Breathless, You and Whose Army? - Radiohead and Dangerous Animals - Arctic Monkeys.

- "What do you call an animal with a prick halfway up its back? A cavalry horse." John's post-dinner chat making the wedding go with a swing.

- We learn that Grace's husbland killed himself, probably after hearing her singing once too often.

- Michael gets a ride off Charlotte, a posh sort from London. Coked off her tits, engaged to a cavalryman and a nose for trouble she seems a real keeper.

- Arthur's best man speech is every bit the lowlight you expect but he does pay moving tribute to his new wife, Linda. She's a woman of faith as you can imagine being married to Arthur. She's a Quaker and he's getting his oats. Everyone's happy.

# Series 3 Episode 2 | The League of Gentlemen

**Bay Six bitch**

Gets around a bit does Thomas Shelby and tonight he's at Lanchester Motor Company in Sparkbrook. He commiserates with night foreman Chris Finch from The Office on the demise of the previous incumbent Mr Nutley who was mysteriously mown down on the train tracks behind the factory. It would be a terrible shame if the new guy were to meet the same fate. So maybe he'd like to hand over the keys to Bay Six in exchange for the very reasonable bribe Tommoi drops in his lap? Finchy acquiesces, like he has a choice. Tommoi's just got that way, you know? Once inside the bay, he inspects the impressive military hardware inside. Armoured vehicles in tiptop condition come under his pitiless gaze. He looks upon them and he is pleased.

**D motherfucker, D**

From there it's a short trip to Charlie Strong's Yard and a meeting with a priest. Don't worry, he hasn't done an Arthur and found God. This is no ordinary cleric. Father John Hughes (Paddy Considine) represents the Economic League or Section D – a shadowy cabal of businessmen, MPs and army brass rather keen to avoid a repeat of the Russian Revolution here in Blighty. There's an arrangement for the League themselves to arrive but they are a no-show. For some reason the prospect of talking in a stinky gypsy yard at five in the morning doesn't appeal to them.

No matter. Father Hughes has some business of his own to discuss with Tommoi. When his orphanage opens he and his buddy Patrick Jarvis MP will be visiting the children regularly. Hearing confession and the like.

"By which I mean putting our cocks in them with great alacrity and vigour, in case you didn't take my meaning."

"Yeah, I got that."

Jesus, Tommoi. WTF? Even for a Catholic this is blatant. As he leaves Hughes gives Tommoi the name of the man he will be meeting at the Ritz Hotel later - Petrovich Romanov. Tommoi actually had plans but he's quickly learning that the never-ending fight against communism does not want to hear about him and his bullshit "plans".

## Do wop

So that means that Tommoi is not present for the important peace meeting with Italian crime boss Vicente Changretta. It's OK though, the brains trust Arthur and John are on the case. Vincent is pissed that the Blinders firebombed the restaurant just to keep his son Angel from attending Tommoi's wedding with Lizzie.

"You tell him from me that my son will walk with any woman in this city."

Well said, old man. And yet John muses that Angel would find walking anywhere a significant challenge if he were to lose his kneecaps. Oh, that's done it. Changretta leaves spitting fire at the slight. Even Arthur looks at John all "Son, I Am Disappoint". The fuck is wrong with that boy?

Polly buttonholes John about the problem later. While it's true that the Blinders run tings, the ritual humiliation of their criminal associates breaches the unwritten code among men of their stripe. To avoid starting a fire Lizzie will break up with Angel and apologise for any frightful inconvenience. John, acting like the touchy prick he increasingly is, flies off the handle and out of the door.

"I'll take his fucking face, how about that?"

Yeah, not really what she had in mind mate. Effing John, man.

## Women's lib(rary)

Once he arrives in London, Tommoi pays a visit to Ada at the British Library. He'd like to do the knowledge on the Russian Revolution, specifically the background of Petrovich Romanov. As he appraises Romanov's entry in the Russian "Who's Screwed" Ada enquires after a Russian of her own. That Anton Kaledin fellow from the wedding. He seemed nice. For some reason Tommoi can't help her with that one. Matchmaking not really his thing.

## Pudding in the Ritz

So when he meets with Romanov in the Ritz Tommoi comes armed with knowledge. Petrovich is not a direct relation to the Romanovs and, despite his grand airs, is more broke than Evander Holyfield. So exactly how does this uppity Georgian hope to pay Tommoi for the very expensive tasks that lie ahead? Romanov assures him that his apparent poverty is but subterfuge designed to garner sympathy from London society. His niece Tatiana personally deposited 49 sapphires in her vagina, one of which he hands over to Tommoi.

"Fucking pongs a bit, right enough."

Breathing in the sweet smell of Russian snatch, Tommoi bids him good day. He's starting to think the Bolsheviks have a point.

**The Italian rob**

Meanwhile, John is busy pouring petrol on the fire he started with the Italians. He ambushes Angel Changretta as he arrives for his suit fitting in Chinatown before BLINDING him in one eye with the razor in his PEAKED cap. Say, I wonder if that might become a thing?

"Stay away from Lizzie!" he shouts, just in case he hasn't got the message.

FFS, John. It seems like he still has a boner for Lizzie Stark, of all women. It's a big relief for Polly and Arthur when Tommoi returns to talk some sense into him and play the pipes of peace. And yet when he makes his ruling it is with the cold cruel eye of the hawk.

"The only way to guarantee peace is by making the prospect of war seem hopeless." he says "If you apologise once, you do it again and again and again, like taking bricks out of the wall of your fucking house."

They'll be hitting back and hard – taking to the Changretta pubs tonight. And why?

"Because we fucking can."

So much for being the cool head of the family.

**Sapphire blew**

How about we catch up with Grace? Having abandoned the life of espionage she plays the gangster's moll with a heart of gold like she was born to it. The upcoming dinner for the

Shelby Charity Foundation will be a real boon for her. Say, why doesn't she wear this ugly hunk of shit sapphire?

"Well, it's a bit tacky. And I'm pretty sure it smells of fanny."

"Grace, this is fucking Birmingham. Good taste is for people who can't afford sapphires."

Yeah, I mean it's only a sapphire at the end of the day. It's not going to kill you!

**Prison chaplain**

So the time comes for the Shelbys to take the Changretta pubs. Arthur is somewhat reluctant, particularly given that Linda is pissing in his ear about the evils of working at night (Testify, sister! - signed, everyone who's ever worked nights). John engages more enthusiastically, embracing the smushing, pummelling and hellraising like a long lost lover. Vincent Changretta meanwhile arranges for a Neapolitan assassin to visit Birmingham. I don't think he's brought him over to show him the canals.

Further trouble arrives in the form of a squad of Scotland Yard rozzers who snatch Tommoi up and dump him in a jail cell. Father Hughes arrives and tells him that deviation from his very specific instructions is not something his associates take kindly to. It's visiting Ada that's the problem.

"Your sister is a potential security breach. She has connections with Bolsheviks in London who have connections with the Soviet Embassy."

Should Tommoi find himself dropping in on the sister again, she'll meet with a fatal road accident. And that Charlie kid? He might be a bit young even for Hughes's tastes but he can get snuffed like *SNAP*. To illustrate this there's a Cooperative Crematorium business card under his pillow marked 'Charles Shelby RIP'. He's not easily rattled but Tommoi is shook. These dudes don't eff about.

## Ruben Oliver

Ruben has been steadily maintaining his semi-boner for Polly all these weeks and he pays her a visit. He'll be painting her in a dress her mother stole while she was a cleaner. He is under the impression that Polly is a "woman of substance and class" rather than, say, a woman of substance abuse and underclass as every available fact would seem to indicate. Still, that's artists for you – an unquenchable desire to be wrong about everything seeing beauty in the mundane every day. Spotting the clear chemistry between the two, Ada forces her to invite him to Grace's charity dinner that evening. Looks like it was meant to be, guys.

## Grace under fire

When the dinner arrives, it's a big success. Grace looks like Marilyn Monroe's hotter younger sister and everyone who's anyone is here. Even the leader of Birmingham City Council attends. Tatiana shows up too, walking a bit more freely now she no longer has 9 kilos of precious stones up her chuff.

Wouldn't you know it though Thomas can't avoid business even on a night like tonight. Father Hughes and Patrick "Paedo" Jarvis MP corner him in the concert hall for discussions on the Russian business. Tommoi will be stealing the military vehicles before transporting them on a train to London. And tomorrow he will be accompanying Tatiana as she inspects the hardware personally. It's just another dumb chore added to his ever-growing list.

Speaking of Tatiana he gets some quality time with the foxy Russian aristo.

"My uncle ordered me to seduce you, to give us an advantage," she tells him "Have you not heard? We have no morals, we Russians."

He likes the sound of that. Less appealing though, is what she tells him next. The sapphire around Grace's neck that until very recently was lodged snugly in her snatch? Cursed by a gypsy.

Pfffffft! Who believes that superstitious nonsense these days? Still, makes you think, particularly when the Neapolitan assassin bursts in and shoots Grace right through the tits. He was aiming for Tommoi but was distracted by the still clear odour of aristocratic Russian quim from the sapphire that hit his olfactory nerve at just the wrong time.

Either that or he's a music lover who heard Grace's singing.

**Notes and observations**

- Musical accompaniment this week courtesy of Crying Lightning by Arctic Monkeys, I Might Be Wrong by Radiohead and This Is Love by PJ Harvey.

- The Grand Duchess Izabella chats with Romanov about Romanov killing Tommoi and the beardie weirdie is totally cool with that. Izabella seems a right dragon. Watch out for her folks.

- "You know, gentlemen, there is hell...and there is another place below hell." Tommoi to the paedo brothers. A bit harsh on Small Heath but pretty accurate to be fair.

- Section D was indeed a shadowy organisation of the time set up by former naval intelligence chief Admiral William Reginald Hall and sundry right-wing wackjobs "to raise sufficient funds to set up an organisation to counter subversion in industry during the critical period of post-war re-adjustment". Nothing in their constitution about hiring gypsies to steal tanks but nothing ruling it out either.

- We are assured that guns don't kill people, people do so who's to blame for Grace copping it? Let's start with John running his mouth and then mutilating his ex's new borefriend. I will only accept the sapphire as a culprit if the bullet bounced off it and went right up her nostril.

# Series 3 Episode 3 | Paint a vulgar picture

## The grieving of Liverpool

So the main news is that Grace is as dead as the chances of Arthur winning Mastermind. A single bullet to the chest blew her Mick norks clean off and rather than have her live the futile sub-existence of a breastless wife Tommoi slapped a Do Not Resuscitate Post-it® note on her forehead and she died peacefully hours later of tit failure. The Widower Shelby has not adjusted well to post-Grace living, sleeping in a field and avoiding his family wherever possible (although to be fair that's pretty reasonable behaviour at the best of times).

But criminal enterprises do not grind to a halt just because some dumb broad gets herself shot. Tommoi calls a series of meetings with family members to set out his grand plan for the near future. He charges Arthur and John with mopping up the remnants of the Italian problem. Angel Changretta is wormfood but his pops Vincent heads that very day to Liverpool whence he will sail to America to see if there's a vacancy for a Mustache Pete.

Snatching up the wop will be simple enough but there's a complication. He travels with Mrs Changretta who was a much beloved schoolteacher of the Shelby boys. It's no complication for Tommoi though who instructs them to ice the dame and throw her body on the ever-growing Pile of Dead Bitches the Peaky Blinders have killed over the past few years.

Arthur and John balk at the thought. Hasn't there been enough death? They are also not crazy about Michael being called in for a meeting first. Since when did that poncey tarted up mummy's boy get priority? What are they to Tommoi – just a couple of thugs? The man himself is unavailable for comment as he has pissed off in a caravan heading to Wales with Johnny Dogs. Well, he's no Grace but he'll do for a while I suppose.

## I recall a gypsy woman

Once he arrives in the land of song, Tommoi's purpose is revealed. He visits with gypsy mystic Bethany Boswell, who runs a bespoke conscience cleaning service. Very exclusive like, only available to those in the know. And the price? One cursed sapphire. As luck would have it Tommoi has just such an item. He prised it from Grace's still-quivering tit the night of her death. Madame Boswell takes the sapphire off his hands and the weight off his mind.

"Bless you, Tommoi Shelby. You'll have good fortune from now on."

He may not be fully on board with the idea of God or any of this black magic savagery but it's still a gypsy heart that beats within his chest. And if ditching the stone is the cost of a simple ritual to allow him to move on, then it's well worth it.

## Factory fodder

Pity poor Finchy. Bad enough that he is a member of the English working class in the West Midlands in the 1920s, born with a face like cunt-caked haggis, he's also got to deal with Arthur and John pissing in his ear. They command him to sack all the members of the South Birmingham Communist Party who work his nightshift. Not big on good labour relations then lads? Finchy is driven to distraction but with the ever present threat hanging over him and his kin he goes along with it. This stopped being fun the moment it started.

## Into Pol

At least Polly's having some fun posing for Ruben so he can make a mess all over his canvas. Still, she can't help but wonder what's in it for him. Is he bragging to his friends about painting a gangster? Does he get some sick thrill from brushing up against the underworld? It turns out it's a little more prosaic than that.

"I am planning to seduce you eventually and, please God, sleep with you."

Polly's never been so insulted in her life. And rarely happier.

## Taking out the trash

The boys abduct Changretta, ignoring Tommoi's very clear instructions to waste his wife. They stick her on the boat to America and tie the wop to a chair for Tommoi's arrival and Changretta's subsequent dismemberment. Once there though Tommoi seems at a bit of a loss where to begin. Tongue? Knackers? Eyeballs? Realising that they will literally be here all night if Tommoi has his way Arthur plugs Changretta in the noggin with a single shot and ends the torture party early. It's for the best.

## Ada aids

Meanwhile, back at Shelby Palace Tommoi is greeted by Ada. She's finally been doing some good work for a change – working her Bolshevik pals to discover a Soviet informant in the Economic League. Tommoi is so grateful for the info he immediately rewards her by offering her the gig of running his Boston operation once he sinks money into the wharfs there. Because nothing says "thank you" like sending someone 3000 miles due west to live in a city of dumb Micks.

## Eat out more often

There's a slap up meal round at Casa Petrovich, hosted by Romanov and the Grand Duchess. Tatiana and Father Hughes also attend. Tommoi won't be staying for long but he does manage to scribble something on a napkin for Izabella. "I have secrets" it says. Exactly what secrets we strictly find out when Tatiana walks into his car.

"The priest is passing information about the robbery to a Lloyd's underwriter called Monkland. He, in turn, is passing information to the Soviet Embassy."

And if the Whites want someone to kill him – well he's their man. He won't be charging a fee for this particular labour of love. It would feel like stealing.

## Notes and observations

- So farewell then Grace. It feels a lot like she was brought back as a show regular just to be slaughtered like a Thanksgiving turkey. It's a way of raising the stakes and increasing the damage to Tommoi whose deathwish will surely only intensify now. That no sense of kinship existed between the pair diminishes the impact somewhat but now we've got Thomas Shelby single dad. Your girlfriend will only want him more.

- A busy music week with Burn the Witch by Queens of the Stone Age, Don't Sit Down 'Cause I've Moved Your Chair by Arctic Monkeys, Tupelo by Nick Cave & The Bad Seeds and Soldier's Things by Tom Waits.

- Arthur's missus Linda is pregnant which means that there is a 50% chance we will have another moustached twat running around the West Midlands being wrong about everything.

- Arthur and John spare Mrs Changretta and then Arthur plugs Mr Changretta before Tommoi can start dismembering him. That's two direct acts of mutiny in one episode. Arthur's getting very brave now he's got his bird's skirts to hide behind.

- Michael continues stoically down the path towards serial killing, enjoying a night time firearms tutorial from Arthur and John. "I'm not a fucking kid any more," he tells an appalled Polly as she tries to break up the party. I'm not sure he ever was.

# Series 3 Episode 4 | The Long Good Friday

**Goodbye to that old hunt**

It is Good Friday. Tommoi takes the boys hunting and informs them of the sad news that their daddy Arthur Shelby senior is dead. The only thing he ever taught them was how to kill and cook a stag and so in his honour they will re-enact his one act of parenting in his miserable shitty life. Before they eat, Tommoi fills them in about the big robbery of the 27 armoured cars. The Whites will pay £150,000, the bulk of which will be reinvested in Boston. After this caper Shelby Ltd will be going completely legit.

"With profits on this scale we'll be in a position to stop the off-track business for good. Keep the pubs, stop the protection. Horses for the sport, race days for the lark."

So just one last job before going legit? I certainly can't think of any instances where that's gone awry in the past.

**Darken the church door**

Polly visits a church to spill her guts to the priest in the confession booth. She tells the priest about the cop she wasted. He says it's a mortal sin but she disagrees citing Moses, Samson and Lord Kitchener for the laffs. In any event, it's not that which bothers her. It's the next chump that the family will be killing.

"He's a man of the cloth. He's a holy man."

To break the Seal of the Confessional is an automatic excommunication in the Catholic Church but yonder priest cares not one jot about that. He grasses Polly up to his buddy Father John "Babyshagger" Hughes, who is very grateful for the intel.

Really great work Polly - even by your standards. She's so pleased with her brilliant stool pigeoning, she decides to further ruin the family's prospects by closing the bookies for the Good Friday racing – one of the busiest days of the year. Instead, she takes the girls to join the strike masterminded by a. They march on the Bull Ring in scenes apparently too offensive to be shown on British television.

**Georgian on my mind**

When Tommoi returns home, he finds Tatiana waiting for him in his chair. She'd rather like proof that Hughes is a traitor. He can't help her with that – merely offering his word – but he can help her with the 3 inches of Birmingham Irish meat she seeks. He shtups her good and proper and leaves her a very happy girl. But he has made his first mistake.

Because Thomas has broken the cardinal rule – never stick your dick in crazy pussy. Tatiana goes apeshit in the middle of the night, laughing like a loon, commandeering his revolver and kicking off a game of Russian Roulette.

"I do not want your mad fucking Russian brains all over my fucking wall." he tells her.

"Did you know that madness sets you free?"

She clearly is not acquainted with section 3 of the Mental Deficiency Act 1913 which states that madness can get you sent to a colony. It's far from a washout though. Apart from the mint posh girl pumpum, he deduces from her babblings that the treasury where the loot is kept is underneath Hampton Court Palace. Arthur has sourced a low-level Russian-Cretan scrote Stefan Radischevky they can place inside the house as a member of staff acting as their eyes and ears. It's pretty clear to Tommoi that they can't trust the Russians to cough up what he's owed so clearing them out is simply giving them what's coming to them.

## Freudian strip

Meanwhile, things are hotting up between Ruben and Polly with the horny painter trying to entice her into his world of Freudian word association. Polly isn't biting for now but she is opening up to him about her celibacy.

"I think when men want sex, they become hilarious." she says, "Like a dog when you pick up a lead."

"IF I'M A DOG, WHAT THAT MAKE YOU?????" he screams silently to himself. The frustration is getting to him.

## Sorry seems to be the hardest word

It's a lovely sunny afternoon – exactly the kind you'd choose if you were fixing to kill a priest. Tommoi follows Father Hughes into the bogs outside a church fete and gets his execution hand ready. Thanks to Polly running her mouth though the paedo gets the jump on him and he and his buddies deliver a ferocious cauliflower arse during their kicking. Permanent brain damage seems likely but Tommoi does retain one important piece of information Hughes passes his way.

"I am passing on information to the Soviet embassy on the instruction of Section D – it's part of a bigger picture."

Tommoi's penance is to attend a dinner at the Russians where he apologises and admits his mistake. He once again threatens to take Charles, reminding him that he can be got at whenever they feel like it.

After he's dumped back home Tommoi starts to make plans – replacing all the staff with gypsies and kin. He tells Ada to hook him up with a meeting with one of her Bolshevik chums from the Soviet Embassy. His next engagement is another awkward dinner at the Ritz with the Romanovs and the paedo MP. Coked off his tits, Tommoi makes his apology. Hughes makes him recite the act of contrition – a humiliating ritual which frankly puts everyone off their stuffed dumplings.

Once that's over with he shoots off to Ada's to meet the Special Adviser to the Soviet Council. Through a translator he tells him that the informant who has told them about the train of armoured vehicles destined for the Whites is working for the bad guys. The Establishment want the Soviets to stop the robbery and commit a violent act on British soil. It will be the Shelbys sacrificed if the Soviets blow up the train. Then diplomatic relations with the Soviets can be broken off and the Government's secret war against communism can go public.

Now he's got that out of his system it's the perfect time to get his ass to a hospital. He's bleeding from every orifice and haemorrhaging internally like Michael Jackson on the eve of a world tour. Sucks to be a Peaky Blinder, man.

## Notes and observations

- Not parent shaming Esme or anything but I'm fairly sure that snorting your weight in coke is a contraindication during pregnancy. It was a different time. You certainly won't see anything like that in Birmingham these days. With the gypsy blood still fiercely coursing through her veins our girl misses the travelling, the tarmac and the open-air. But most of all the cocaine.

- "John says the girl looks like Edna Purviance from the pictures". A bit insulting to Tatiana. Although Edna was considered a great beauty, Tatiana is way hotter than that.

- Jessie Eden was a real figure in labour relations in Birmingham although Stephen Knight takes some dramatic license with the dates. The working man's struggle often pops up in Peaky Blinders although, unlike Ada, none of the brothers give a rat's ass about it.

- Linda is planning to reform Arthur "to the absolute degree of redemption" which is an ambitious task certainly. The gigantic payday she haggles from the upcoming grand larceny will oil those wheels significantly. She is no mug for a Quaker. She plans to take him to California to run a general store while she works on a mission civilising the Native Americans.

- So Ada has a scholar's pass for the British Library? Who did she steal that from?

# Series 3 Episode 5 | What's it all about, Alfie?

**Tunnel vision**

Tommoi recuperates in hospital, hallucinating flashbacks to a tunnel collapse during the war. A little light brain surgery has helped his recovery along and oral morphine and opium pipes get him through the worst. Michael visits him with some intel on Father Hughes. It seems that after Polly beat off stiff competition to be worst mother in Small Heath in the year 1905 Michael was taken into care where he encountered the good father many times and the strong feeling is that the encounters were neither brief nor sweet. If the priest must die then Michael wants to be the one who does it. Tommoi will give it some thought.

Three months down the line, Tom has finally exhausted Western Europe's supply of morphine and decides to get back in the game. It's a tough decision but the vision of Maid Mary reciting the Bible bollock naked by his bed lets him know that even grim reality is better than his hopped up dreams.

## The factory

The ever shifting ground on which the fragile alliances are made and broken takes the Soviets along to Bay 6 of the factory with the Blinders. They remove the firing pins from the tanks to sabotage the vehicles. Now there's no need for the Soviets to blow up the train.

"And I'll tell Tommoi you accept his plan," says Arthur.

I wonder what plan this is? I'll wager it's something to do with the robbery. He instructs Johnny Dogs to take his travelling hordes to land just outside Hampton Court Palace where Tommoi has just bought the land. It'll be a nice cover for the tunnelling they'll need to do.

## King of the jewels

There's also an unexpected conference with Alfie Solomons. He makes a heartfelt apology to Arthur for all that unpleasantness down in London so business can begin. But Alfie being Alfie he can't help but mock Arthur's new-found Christianity. It's not enough that they killed Christ – Jews have to keep on badmouthing him until the Day of Judgment when they will be cast into the fiery pit. Arthur grasps a nearby ashtray to cave his skull in with but thinks better of it. He accepts his apology like a true Christian luckily for everyone concerned.

## Don't get your Hampton caught

The tragedy is that they need the filthy Heeb to do some verification and costing over at Hampton Court. Who knows the price of everything better than a Jew? During the traditional strip search, Princess Tatiana jerking off Arthur in front of Tommoi gives the boy a pang of jealousy. He has time to work through that during the vodka and hookers orgy that follows.

John breaks off from the merrymaking to make contact with Stefan Radischevky the man on the inside.

"It's a fucking madhouse!" the scrote informs him "The Prince wants me to suck his cock."

He's probably had worse offers. In other news he has learned that the strongroom is guarded at night and that the Romanovs plan slaughtering the three brothers with machine guns once their business is concluded. Standard.

They all check out the Treasury together under the guise of making sure that the jewellery is bona fide though naturally Tommoi is casing the joint from the inside. Tatiana invites Tommoi to choose jewels worth £70,000 that will constitute his fee.

And what jewels. There's a necklace from Czar Nicholas himself, a diamond vibrator and, the coup de grace, a giant Fabergé egg the Grand Duchess has been keeping in her cavernous vagina for just such an occasion. The booty is fully assembled. It will be kept in a box and delivered to Tommoi on successful execution of his mission.

**The horror, the horror**

The painting is now completed and Polly is invited over for a private viewing. She barely recognises the regal, sexually attractive woman staring back at her from the canvas. So with all that tiresome painting business over with all that's left for these two is to have depressing futile geriatric sex and they do exactly that. No love is more disgusting than old love and I'm including Cleveland Steamers and whatever it is pet players get up to. Polly's attempts to spice things up and make this unholy rattling mass of calcium somehow enticing include spilling all about the time she killed Campballs. It's a huge failure just like her life. Effing Polly man.

## Mole men

Tommoi assembles his crew of tunnel diggers from the war among the new Gypsy Lee settlement by Hampton Court. Say hello to the Tipton Clay Kickers - good men, every one of them. He gives them the skinny on the caper and they are ready to go. The war may have taken their innocence and their sanity but the skills learned in those unforgiving shitpits are going to set them up for life.

## Mother stands for comfort

Doing a passable impersonation of a concerned mother Polly snoops around in Michael's desk and finds a bullet with the priest's name on it. She confronts Tommoi who tells her that the priest molested her boy to within an inch of his life when she was busy drinking gin and sucking failed bank robber cock. A solitary tear of remorse, shame and regret rolls down her 300-year-old face. She totally gets it. Michael has every right to his revenge. Nonetheless, she has this to say.

"I swear to God if my son pulls the trigger I will bring this whole fucking organisation down around your ears."

And you know why? Because Tommoi doesn't have the right to let him.

## Notes and observations

- That's David Bowie's Lazarus playing as Tommoi re-enters the world of the living. Truly, he is The Prettiest Star.

- Michael has got that broad Charlotte pregnant and the general feeling is that abortion is the way forward. Like we need another Shelby in the world.

- Ada is now officially the new Head of Property and Acquisitions. Her transition from communist to capitalist is now complete.

- "You people, you hunted my mum with dogs through the snow." Alfie explaining to the Romanovs how he came to speak Russian and bear grudges.

- Stefan may currently be contemplating sucking Imperial cock currently but there is the pub of his dreams waiting for him when he's done. Everyone makes sacrifices.

# Series 3 Episode 6 | Mr Egg – Eat like a king for £1 million

## Always the last place you look

Gangsters have a long tradition of distracting people from their tyranny with philanthropy and the Shelbys are certainly all about that today. It's the grand opening of the Grace Shelby Institute for Orphaned Children.

"These children are safe." says Tommoi in his keynote speech "In our care they will be safe because we are from the same cold streets they are. And in our care they won't be shipped away to the colonies, not separated from kin or made to work for men in the various ways."

It's stirring stuff and the Stalinist standing ovation is but a formality, particularly with Arthur menacing everyone into rising. So it's with impeccable timing that Father Hughes arrives to take over his rape suite. The Shelby orphans will be visiting St Aloysius's with great regularity he informs him, and seeing more unwelcome sex than a Bill Cosby co-star. It puts a real damp squib on things as Tommoi mixes with the dignitaries.

But mix he must and it suddenly seems like everyone wants a piece of him. Pressing the flesh and hobnobbing with the quality are part of the deal and a dizzying stream of well-wishers and wankers flows over him to backslap and bear hug. In all the excitement he mislays Charlie but it's nothing to worry about. I mean, it's not like there was a very recent threat to abduct him by a sociopath paedophile who he was talking to only minutes bef- Ah...

Panic reigns as Tommoi hares around the building in search of his son but the truth his bones already knows descends on him horribly like a fat girl sitting on an old man's face. Charlie has been taken - by the worst people in the universe.

## The negotiations

Like the thoughtful soul he is, Father Hughes picks Tommoi up personally in his motor. The Padre knows about his dalliance with the Soviets and his plan to double cross them. That's why Charlie is currently MIA and DTF (whether he likes it or not).

"You have all the cards," says Tommoi desperately "Tell me what you want me to do and I will certainly do it."

What Tommoi will be doing is blowing up the train himself, killing half a dozen poor sods in the process, and scattering fragments to implicate officials from the Soviet embassy. The Reds will be taking a PR hit one way or another. Oh and that Lilies of the Valley egg he'll be nicking from the Russians? That now goes to one of the Odd Fellows' wives who has a bit of an obsession with Fabergé. The rest of the booty will go to the Economic League leaving Tommoi potless with some seriously pissed off tunnellers to placate. It's raining in Birmingham and raining in his heart. Today makes the first day of the Somme look like a sunny walk in the park.

## A family affair

Even as his head spins one thing is clear as day to Tommoi. His organisation is leaking like your dad's anal fissures and someone very close to him has been running their mouth. Only Arthur, John, Ada and Polly knew about the egg and when he gets them all together he starts musing out loud which one of them blabbed. Maybe Linda through Arthur or Esme through John? A Soviet triple agent through Ada? And what about that Ruben twat who's been sticking it to Polly?

"He sought you out. Why would an educated man of his standing do something like that?"

He's done the odds and it's 50:50 everything is Polly's fault. A harsh but fair appraisal on both the current crisis and her life in general.

## Throw the Jew down the well

From there Thomas has some business with Alfie whom he meets in one of the many disused warehouses available for such nefarious rendezvous. Alfie is there to provide Tommoi with a list of men of means married to women with a boner for Fabergé eggs. But when he hands over the list it's like a Jackson 5 family photo – there's one missing. Tommoi knows this having already done the knowledge with his people in the Jewellery Quarter. Alfie's duplicity reveals him as the leak. I dunno, man. It's like you can't trust criminals any more.

But come on – crime's crime but a kid's been abducted. Alfie crossed a line. As the pair tussle Alfie's bodyguard wrestles Tommoi away and gets his head blown off by Michael who loses his kill virginity with the minimum of fuss. Alfie looks in deep shit right now but instead of begging for his life he decides to go on the offensive.

"How many sons have you cut, killed, murdered, fucking butchered – innocent and guilty?"

After some reflection Tommoi has to admit he's got a point. They leave to catch up with this Gilbert Palmer guy who he left off the list. Coppers on the Blinders payroll pick him up at his home and bring him into a prison cell where Arthur and John await to interrogate him into a more voluble state than he is currently comfortable with. They may not be the brightest but they do have their uses.

## All art is quite useless

The idea that Ruben has been playing her sends Polly into a tailspin. Six bottles of gin later, she breaks into Ruben's gaff and slashes the portrait to ribbons. She's no Brian Sewell but she knows what she likes. When Ruben arrives she sticks an Uzi in his face demanding answers. He protests his innocence and there's something about him that rings true. Maybe it's the near lethal levels of alcohol in her system or just that she is old and horny but she tosses her gun away and pashes with him like he's the last painter on earth.

## The tunnel

There's no rest for the wicked and Tommoi currently has the schedule of POTUS, the Pope and Bill Gates combined. The news from the tunnel is that they've hit heavy clay and that it's about as likely to finish on time as a child star is to reach their 21st birthday. Notwithstanding his crippling fear of tunnels, he heads down there himself to aid with the effort, spearheading the digging, face first like a psychotic mole. They're running low on timber and with water making the tunnel unstable only a madman would continue. On he presses, risking everything.

Because Tommoi's a gambling man and if he loses Charlie he may as well be dead anyway. He's done the odds. Two sticks of gelignite take out the last of the clay. The tunnel survives the blast – barely, swaying and crumbling but still there. Nearly passing out with exhaustion he grabs all the eggs and jewels he can and GTFO like he just stole something.

Which, of course, he has.

## Charlie is our darling

Having loosened Gibson's tongue along with his bowels and several of his ribs Arthur and John hand over Charlie's likely location to Michael. They send two experienced killers with him for the rescue attempt but now his blood is up Michael feels like he can kill anyone. When they arrive at the location he orders the lunks to stay in the car. He follows the sounds of Charlie's sobs and comes face-to-face with his abuser. His hand shakes as he raises his weapon. Hughes easily disarms him and sets about choking him into another dimension. Luckily Michael has a pocketknife handy and sticks it right in his eye. He then cuts the priest's throat, damn near decapitating him in the process. I don't think he'll be making it to series 4. Looks like Charlie will be though. Nicely done Michael, you posh twat.

## The grave train

As the workers call their wildcat strike at the factory the Blinders enter. Arthur tells them that the locomotive carrying the armoured vehicles will be meeting with an unfortunate accident. If they hear nothing by 10 PM then the train will be blown up with John and Arthur laying the charges on the line and doing the detonating.

They wait eagerly for news from Finn about Charlie. The message comes just a second too late. They blow the train and six good men to kingdom come. The heads, arms and legs of the damned rain down on the tracks. Bad lucks guys!

**Why have cotton when you can have silk?**

And so the fearful Russian business ends on a road out in the sticks where Tommoi meets with Tatiana. Along with a suitcase full of dollars for Tommoi, she has brought along Mr Silk, a jeweller, to check that the stolen loot is kosher. Tatiana will be taking the stash, fucking over her family and heading to Vienna where a man waits for her.

"You needed a tunnel, I needed your signature to make this sale legal." Tommoi says.

Ah so Tatiana was in on it all along. She's a piece of work right enough. There's just time for one last make out before she sends him away with an open invite to look her up in Vienna if he's ever passing. To underline that it would be a really terrible idea she blows Mr Silk's head off in a rather rigged game of Russian Roulette.

What have we told you about crazy pussy, Tommoi?

# Can't fight City Hall

Once that's been attended to there's the matter of tying up family business. It's been a testing time to say the least and Tommoi gathers his clan in his office for some soothing words backed up with large wads of cash. He's sorry about the literal and figurative train wreck of the Russian adventure even though he had precisely zero choice in the whole sorry episode. He's sorry about doubting Linda, Ada, (less so what's-his-face who's sticking his cock in Polly).

And when Polly tries to stop him giving Michael his bung for offing the priest that's when Tommoi kicks off.

"Those bastards are worse than us. Politicians, fucking judges, lords and ladies, they are worse than us and they will never admit us to their palaces no matter how legitimate we become because of who we are and where we're fucking from."

And you know how he knows? Because even as he speaks the Establishment move against them. The previous night Moss told Tommoi that warrants have been issued for Polly for the murder of Campballs, John and Arthur for the explosion and Michael for Hughes. But it's OK, Tommoi has a plan which he can only hint at in the vaguest terms as uniforms burst into his home and take his family away. Their enemies do not control the elected government he tells them.

"I have made a deal in return for giving evidence against them," he continues, "It's all taken care of."

He assures them that he's made a deal with people "even more powerful than our enemies". And you know Tommoi. He's done the odds.

Our boy is left alone like Michael Corleone at the end of the Godfather II with only ghosts and an annoying child for company. He looks the loneliest man alive.

**Notes and observations**

- The Lilies of the Valley Fabergé egg was made in 1898 in the Art Nouveau style. These days the egg would set you back about £10 million. Of the 50 eggs Fabergé designed three remain missing, eagerly sought out by fanatical bozos.

- Radiohead make another appearance in the Peaky Blinders canon with Life In A Glass House.

- It's a good thing that Tatiana survived the season finale. That crazy bitch is a huge amount of fun. We can but hope that she becomes Irene Adler to Tommoi's Sherlock. She thinks she understands him. That makes one of her.

- Exceptional work by Tom Hardy here – his moral relativist monologue stopping the murderous Tommoi in his tracks. It's good to see Tommoi called on his bullshit once in a while and no one does it with more style and clarity than the wandering Jew.

- A lot of the good work in the First World War was done underground and the Tipton Claykickers here representing the heroic tunnelling squads of the Allies, set up by John "Hellfire Jack" Norton-Griffiths.

# Series 4 Episode 1 | Should have killed me last year

## Hangmen

The more things change, the more they stay the same. They may have survived the Russian Revolution, the cursed sapphire and the baby raping cleric but the Shelbys are still taking it up the pipe. Arthur, Michael and John are dragged out of their prison cells and unceremoniously dumped by a hangman's scaffold. Made-to-measure nooses dangle above them. In a few seconds they will be hanged by the neck until dead in the storied tradition of summary executions passim. In better news, Polly gets exactly the same treatment at Winson Green Clink for Dicey Old Broads. Who is behind this outrage? How did things get so complicated? And where the frigging feck is Tommoi?

No one seems to be quite sure but he is being spoken about in high places. The monarch's private secretary Arthur Bigge is told to WhatsApp the king that very instant so he can intervene on behalf of Tommoi. Is he for real? George V has a hectic globetrotting schedule. Why the hell would he be interested in some subhuman bluenose scrotes in England's bleakest city? Well, the handwritten letter from the king Tommoi has in his possession could certainly help with that. It reads:

*"Dear Grand Duke Romanov*

*I am writing to congratulate you on your continuous struggle to fight the Soviet regime. My support is ever-growing.*

*I believe the explosion of the railroad was a truly magnificent operation! I can guarantee our support hereon.*

*Yours George R, of Houses Windsor and Spitzlgruber,*

*Fifth of His Name, King of the Andals and the First Men,*

*Lord of the Seven Kingdoms, and Protector of the Realm"*

Well, looks like someone in the Palace was watching Peaky Blinders series three closely.

"How the fuck did a Birmingham racketeer get his hands on a personal letter written by King George?" wonders Arthur.

Well, quite. It turns out that Tommoi robbed Hampton Court (of course he did). And while he hates to blackmail the Crown or anything, if his family aren't released immediately then he will be releasing proof of the King's sundry nefarious doings and almost certainly starting World War II in the process. So from the outside looking in, kind of seems he has leverage, no?

You can only hope word doesn't reach prison before Polly is executed. With the noose firmly tightened around her neck, she whispers an entreaty to her saviour.

"Lord Jesus, with this rope pull me up to heaven."

I dunno, man. After murdering Campballs and the Birmingham accent all these years I think Polly may be headed somewhere significantly warmer. Either way we won't be finding out just yet as the inevitable last minute reprieve comes in the last minute with a minute to go in the final 60 seconds of Fergie time. The non-existent tension is relieved. Now we can get on with the show.

**It's an honour**

♪ *Christmas time! Mistletoe and Wine! Sex with hookers because you're dead inside.*♫

We fast forward to one year later, 23 December 1925. Tommoi Shelby has been awarded an OBE, for services to Blackmailing the Crown, an honour richly deserved and well earned. Don't anticipate him being deluged with congratulations telegrams from family members though. The Shelbys are very much a family going their separate ways these days.

Tommoi's living out of the Midland Hotel, rocking John Lennon specs and numbing the PTSD pain with casual sex and cocktails. Lizzie comes up to his table to tell him about the great New Year's party over at John's this year. It would be great if he could just show up and clear the air after all that unpleasantness (specifically, his entire life and that of his entire shitty family). The children will keep everyone in check she assures him.

"You can't pull a razor with a baby there, not even Esme."

Tommoi delivers a hard no. New Year's Eve, he's busy fucking some prostitute to death. Lizzie is truly disgusted – mainly because he chose another sex worker over her but also because he's been acting out like this ever since the end of series three. What has got into him? He can't live another year like this.

"Sex, freedom, whiskey sours – which one should I give up first?"

Well, when you put it like that.

## Down to the wire

But we all know that it's business that really gives Tommoi the horn. It may be Christmas Eve but he charges down to Shelby Company Ltd to sort out a bit of union trouble. Michael tells him that a local union convener says they are underpaying the female wirecutters just because they are ladies. The nerve! Tommoi is the biggest employer of working girls in the city, as a look at his hotel bill will confirm. That Jessie Eden broad name checked in the last series is the high-grading aggregator causing trouble. Tommoi will attend to her personally and we know what that usually means.

He does take time out to coke shame Michael for his 3 ounce a day habit and hit him up for intell on Polly. It turns out she's got even more annoying since her near death experience. She's on pills for her nerves like Bobby Chariot and is giving séances to imbeciles. Not for the first time or the last, Tommoi regrets saving his family from the noose.

## Shelbyville

So just how are the rest of the Shelbys as Christmas approaches? Polly is insane and talking to her drowned daughter and John is shooting at innocent birds as Ada rolls up to promote a new Pax Shelby for the New Year. Esme pooh-poohs that idea with her 493rd gypsy curse of the year. She is hoping to reach 500 before Big Ben chimes in 1926. In these challenging times, it's good for a homemaker to have a hobby.

"They put a noose around his neck – he shat himself!" she tells Ada of John's near death experience. It's the kind of comment the phrase "too much information" was invented for.

Beating a hasty retreat, Ada's next journey is to Arthur's farm where our favourite moustached simpleton plays with his son Billy as he is brutally pussywhipped to within an inch of his life by his hateful god-bothering wife Linda. Ada will be very happy to get back to America after dealing with these sacks of shit.

**First cutter's the deepest**

Over at Shelby Company Ltd, Tommoi receives the notorious union convener Jessie Eden (Charlie Murphy). He's done his background on her and has uncovered that she is a sexually attractive woman. She in turn has done her background on Tommoi Shelby and the smoke and mirrors paper trail that links his business empire together. As they swap industrial relations themed barbs it is clear it is just a prelude to him putting his cock in her. She wants parity. As it so happens, he has a solution to that.

"I will increase the pay of the female cutters in this factory by five shillings and I will cut the pay of the male cutters in the Rover by five shillings thereby achieving your sacred fucking parity."

Oh Tommoi, you terrible cunt! But this Jessie Eden broad is no pushover. She was prepared for exactly this outcome.

"My comrade brothers and sisters are not afraid of you, Mr Shelby. I will call an extraordinary meeting of my executive committee as soon as Boxing Day. You will hear the whistles blow all across Birmingham."

Suck on that, you capitalist fuck. That should give him something to think about over Christmas.

## Play your cards – right?

Yeah, about that. Given that he has no friends, no girlfriend and everyone in his family hates him, it's looking like a pretty sparse Christmas Day round at Casa Shelby. With that in mind, he sends invites to 27 people - Johnny Dogs and his crew of gypsy psychopaths mostly. Sounds like one for the ages (the Dark Ages).

The thing about Christmas though, is to reach out and reconnect with the important people in your life. Tommoi receives a lovely Christmas card all the way from America from one Luca Changretta. Look – it's got a black hand on and everything! I wonder if he's any relation to the late Angel Changretta blinded by John and that Vicente Changretta guy they tortured and murdered before letting his wife free last season? Hm.

Back at Casa Pussywhipped, the conversation is really hotting up. Ada tells them all about Boston and how it's just a shit Birmingham, like Manchester. With Arthur too terrified to talk, Linda tells Ada everything he's been up to.

"He does voluntary work. He drives old people and cripples."

Fortunately, this spectacularly tedious conversation is interrupted by a phone call from John to tell them that they are at war with the "fucking Sicilian Mafia". They've been served the black hand too.

Arthur shits himself, like John did on the scaffold. For a family of ruthless gangsters they really are a bunch of pussies. He passes it on to Ada who makes Tommoi her next port of call.

## Arrival

As all that goes on, dark clouds gather in the north. At the Liverpool docks, there is a filthy stink and it's not just the pong from the tenements. A group of olive oil smelling Italians enter the country headed by Luca Changretta. The customs officer stops him to ask where he's going with that large unwieldy weapon.

"That's my nose you cunt," he responds.

"Beg your pardon, sir. Enjoy your stay."

It's a gigantic fucking hooter right enough. Good luck keeping that under wraps.

## Mommie dearest

They may never be a mom more shit than Polly. Jesus Christ but she is terrible. As Michael visits, he probably realises this. Bottles of Captain Morgan's pile eight-deep by the fireplace, dirty knickers are strewn all over the living room and he's fairly certain that's a puddle of piss slowly soaking into the carpet. She briefly regains enough lucidity to ask him to pass on a vital Christmas message to Tommoi

"Fuck off."

These attempts at reconciliation really aren't panning out.

But still. It's Christmas Eve! Ada arrives at Tommoi's. His brilliant strategy to avoid the incoming slaughter is to gather all the Shelbys in one place where they would never dare take them on.

"Woi wanna be together!" he says as Ada facepalms.

They agree that the Shelbys will once again live within a four-mile radius of the Garrison, just like the old days. There will be a family meeting to confirm the details. And we know how those always go so well.

## Pasta chef

The very last thing Tommoi needs right now is some trifling issue with the domestic staff but that's what he gets. His new chef Jacomo Goodfella keeps on asking when the guests will be coming to Christmas dinner. His sous chef Fucky Luciano is a bit feisty too. They've got him peeling spuds which is something of a comedown given his skills. These Italians!

It could be the whiskey sours talking but something about this doesn't sit right with Tommoi. He goes downstairs to the kitchen is to have a chat, introduce himself and check everything is above board. These greaseballs give no eff and Tommoi's suspicions only increase. He freaks the old chef right the fuck out and goes pretty hard-core with his threats. Inevitably, the old geezer caves. It's true, he worked at one of Darby Sabini's old joints in London and he was only obeying orders.

"They just said bring him here…" he confesses.

The fake sous chef Antonio chooses this moment to make his move, earning himself a meat hook through the tits and a bullet through the brain for his troubles. As for the old fuck, Tommoi has some good news. He's going to let him live on the condition that he delivers a message to Darby Sabini. He picked the wrong side in this war, just like he will in 1939.

Yeah, but who's gonna cook Christmas dinner now, genius? Effing Tommoi man.

## Country life (and death)

All this bloodshed has really accelerated the schedule for that vital family meeting. Arthur is told to GTFO to Small Heath, Polly and Ada are taken to Charlie's yard, it's only John no one can seem to contact. Tommoi sends Michael to rouse his truculent brother. It is the following morning before he can get there and the journey is only half the problem. On Christmas morning, the very last thing John wants to do is to have a bullshit family meeting with his bullshit brothers about their bullshit vendetta. What Michael should do is come inside, have an eggnog and forget about all his troubles. All of a sudden Our Lady of Famous Last Words, Esme, appears with a Christmas message.

"Tell Tommoi Shelby we can look after ourselves!"

You think? There's a handful of heavily armed Italian-Americans hiding behind those hay bales who would beg to differ with that. As they open fire with their machine guns filling John with more holes than Swiss cheese, no amount of gypsy curses can help Esme or save her dopey husbland. Michael's leaking claret from a few slugs as well. Looks like these "Mafia" guys aren't playing around.

Merry fucking Christmas, everyone.

## Notes and observations

- If anyone should die, it should be John as the war with the Changrettas was entirely his fault. He couldn't stand to see Lizzie date an Italian and started maiming made men - generally a path that ends badly. So screw him, basically.

- "Keep her off the fucking snow" is wise counsel with regard to Polly, although "keep her off the fucking show" would be even better.

- Tommoi asking Lizzie what he got Charlie's for Christmas is a Godfather II reference. Tom Hagen tells Michael what he got his son Anthony for Christmas ("It was a little car with an electric motor that he can ride in. It's nice.")

- "Vaffanculo!" Fans of Romanzo Criminale will know this particular curse, littered liberally throughout that show. It's the last thing shit-for-brains sous chef ever says so be careful where you deploy it, yeah?

- We learn that Arthur would like to open a garage so there's your spin-off when Peaky Blinders finally runs out of gas.

# Series 4 Episode 2 | Beacon bingo

**Hex offender**

Chaos reigns. A badly wounded Michael is rushed to hospital and things don't look good. Polly's never looked good and looks even worse now. Her son is leaking blood like a fucking colander and has a face with the pallor of a Scottish girl's arse. Looking a lot better is John, so peaceful and serene. Being dead like a little bitch will do that to you. As he lies there in the morgue stiff as a Michelle Dockery performance, Arthur is particularly upset that they shot him on his doorstep as if that were some particularly egregious insult.

They stand over his body and note that he has shat himself, once again. It's how he would have wanted to be remembered. Defecating himself like a ras claat. Tommoi tries to get John to recite "in the bleak midwinter" for some reason. We will return to that.

It looks like there may be another murder incoming as the hysterical Esme runs in to put a fatal pounding on Tommoi. Fortunately he is able to get the crazy bitch in a rear-naked chokehold to subdue her psychotic rage, for now at least. Like the thieving bastard she is, she steals all John's jewellery, after all what the fuck is he gonna do with it? Everyone has their own way of dealing with grief and for Esmeralda it is to revert to what she knows best.

"No peace for either of you...ever!"

Tell us something we don't know, doll.

**Arms and the man**

Bereavement gets everybody stating the obvious. In an impressive addition to the "no shit, Sherlock" canon, Tommoi addresses the family and lets them know the situation they are in

"John is dead, Esme's gone on the road with the Lees – she's taken the kids, Michael is badly wounded."

Say what you see, Tommoi. There's a vendetta against the Shelbys and la cosa nose-tra won't rest until every ignorant Small Heath piece of shit joins John in Hell. Arthur calls dibs on killing Changretta, him being the older brother and everything. He's even had a bullet specially made with LUCA engraved on it – how adorable! Even in the midst of gang war, it's the little touches that count.

Tommoi predictably is more concerned with the practicalities. He tells the family to squash their internal beef and stay close to the Blinders strongholds of Small Heath, Bordesley Green and the Watering Hole. This is no ordinary criminal skirmish. To fight the Mafia, he will have to recruit some of the worst people in the universe. He's going to hit up Aberama Gold.

"Tommoi, his people are fucking savages," says Johnny Two Dogs, a man named after his parents.

Kind of the point old boy. A busy period of rearmament follows with revolvers, Glock 9s and Uzis handed out like Christmas presents to the Blinders' soldiers.

# My big fat gypsy funeral

A moving gypsy ceremony is held for John. In the eulogy, Tommoi explains how he, John, Arthur, Danny Whizz-Bang, Freddie Thorne, Lenny Henry, Ozzy Osbourne, Lee Hendrie, Benny from Crossroads, Jasper Carrott, Mister Egg and Jeremiah were stuck in a small boat in town called Shit's Creek waiting for the Prussian cavalry to arrive and disembowel them. As they waited, Jeremiah insisted that they sing "In the bleak midwinter". The rest is history. The Prussians never came, they escaped with their arses intact and returned to make the world a worse place for the Garrison Lane widows, the Custard Factory weirdos and everybody else they came across. Now John Shelby will be burned in a gypsy caravan just like he would have wanted.

Tell you what though it's a bit of a risk they are taking out here in this field. If you didn't know better, you'd imagine that Tommoi set this up deliberately to smoke out the filthy Sicilians. As it happens, that's exactly how it is. Two of their number lay in wait to make this a three-for-the-price-of-one Shelby funeral. The greaseball assassin takes aim. Tommoi is in his sights.

"Say your prayers, you ignorant fucking Nose," whispers the Sicilian "Up the Villa!"

It's looking like curtains for Tommoi but just then Johnny Garlicbread is garrotted and kebabed by a striking-looking Irishman. Team Greaseball are shot one by one through the face. Say hello to Aberama Gold (Aidan Gillen). He's that impossibly topical savage you've been hearing about.

"You put us out in the open on purpose," says Polly to Tommoi, always on hand for an exposition dump, "Used John's funeral fire as a fucking beacon!"

Polly is in a strange place at the moment and I'm not talking about a gigantic stinky field littered with the still quivering corpses of Italian assassins. In what passes for her mind, she is the conscience of the family, even though it is apparent to everyone that she's just some pissed old lush with a bug up her crack.

In any event, the bodies are wrapped up and put on a barge to send a message to the Mafia, the message being "Look, bab – there's two stinky dead Italians for yer! LOL!"

FFS, Tommoi.

**Aussie rules**

It's been a full 36 minutes since Polly had a drink so she heads off to ICU at the General Hospital where she immediately divests the bodyguards of their Jack Daniels. That's her drinking sorted for the weekend and even though she is the worst mother in history, she figures she may as well pay a visit to Michael while she's there and she has a fantastic proposal for him. The two of them will go away to the up-and-coming penal colony they are calling Australia. She's got a magazine about it and everything. When she learns to read it will no doubt be very instructive.

"There are no Italians in Australia," she says.

"I think there are, mom," he replies.

Jesus Christ, she's one dumb sack of shit. Still, Michael does agree to go with her as long as she stays strong during this crisis and reduces her alcohol intake to 800 cl of scotch a day, deliberately including a condition she has no hope of sticking to.

# The Gold standard

Back in the city of Birmingham, Aberama and his goons pay a visit to Uncle Charlie's yard. He makes a polite enquiry as to the yard's asking price. A visibly shaken Charlie tells him it's not for sale but it simply doesn't convince. I mean, everyone's got a price and Charlie's may be whatever makes this terrible sense of impending doom whenever this little weirdie walks past go away.

You get the feeling this Aberama guy isn't used to being told no. He raises the yard issue with Tommoi who has a proposal for him. They spin a coin for it.

"If it's heads, Abby here takes all of this...with my blessing. And if it's tails I fuck your daughter, Mr Gold."

"LOL, you seen her though blud? Good luck with that one."

Nonetheless, Tommoi appears quite serious. It's time for Aberama to back down.

"Tommy Shelby, OBE – no wager today but with this penny I will buy a flower to put on your grave - when the time comes".

Well, that turned nasty quickly. I thought we were all pals?

An alfresco dinner shortly follows with Polly, Lizzie and Ada joining the boys. Polly tells Tommoi that ever since the noose incident that she's just like him and Arthur – drunk and hairy. Everything from now on is a bonus.

"When you're dead already, you're free."

But mostly dead. Of course, Tommoi wants her back in the clan and she is on board with that because Michael wants it.

She immediately gets to work with some surprisingly common sense advice on the realities of wartime business.

"Get your whores vetted by Lizzie - they'll use your weakness. Don't take any new men on in the factories unless you know their families."

She also tells him how to deal with Aberama Gold. She suggests he should be asking what he really wants. And so, like a little bitch, Tommoi immediately runs off to Aberama and asks him what he really wants. The weirdie responds by asking his son Bonnie to take off his shirt so Tommoi can fulfil his dream.

"Look, I'm flattered but I don't do bummers," he responds, "Only whores - really skanky ones. Have you met Lizzie?"

It turns out that sodomy is not part of the deal, at least not for now. We'll get to that.

**Seeing red**

It's been a while since Linda entertained a gentleman caller in the dead of night but in the wee hours that's exactly what happens. Inspector Moss is the gentleman in question and he's come to pass on some intell about the seven intelligence service officers on their way to Birmingham from London.

"They've got a list of people of great interest and top of that list is Ada Thorne, formerly Shelby."

This can only be good news. It's about time someone sorted out that filthy Communist as we all know Tommoi won't.

## Fighting talk

For one thing, he may have the distraction of an old flame. You think he's just all about the whores and the whiskey but when May Fitz-Carleton shows up at the yard she's looking just as smoking as ever. She's come to "pick up" Tommoi's "horse" which disappointingly can be taken literally in this instance. Give it time.

Right now though, he has a few issues at the foundry. Tommoi brings Bonnie Gold to the factory. It seems he has ambitions of being a boxer and Tommoi knows just the guy to beat that out of him. Billy Mills, factory worker and former boxer. He's a handy enough pug right enough. 75 to the jaw of this young idiot should persuade him that boxing is the mug's game Chris Eubank will one day correctly tell everyone it is. Bonnie may have 20 years on the old twat but Billy outweighs him by about 17 stone. This will be an easy fight.

Well of course it is but not for Billy. It is Bonnie who finishes triumphant knocking out the ancient imbecile with very little difficulty. It looks like the Blinders are entering the sports management business. Why let a little thing like being under existential threat stop you from expanding?

## The union forever

A greater enemy than a man trying to punch you in the balls awaits though. Tommoi meets with Jessie Eden in his office again. She's here to tell him that his dick swinging negotiating tactics won't work post-Russian Revolution.

"I have it on very good authority that Bolsheviks couldn't organise a fucking picnic," he tells her bitterly remembering series three.

That may be true but they did organise a history altering revolution – there's always that. His salty attitude makes her blow her whistle and bring the men out on strike. He really should have seen that coming.

**Monologuing twat**

Next up is his 2 o'clock, which seems routine enough – a delegate for the European Council for Trade. His name is Pierre Surrender and he comes across like Officer Crabtree from 'Allo 'Allo. Weird thing is he looks a lot like Luca Changretta but that's only because he is. With a mind as sharp as Tommoi's it is not long before he has his weapon drawn. No, not like that - his firearm, which he points at his brother's murderer. I'd like to see him get out of this one!

"During the trouble you had earlier on your factory floor," says Changretta "I sent an accomplice into your office in overalls. He found your gun and unloaded it."

"Ah balls..."

Fortunately for Tommoi he hasn't come to, say, kill him and all his family but rather to TELL him that he's going to kill him and his family. Which he already knew. As redundant supervillain monologuing goes, it's certainly up there.

"Your level of security is pitiful," he says, giving him a much-needed heads up.

They agree on some rules of combat. No civilians, no children and no politics.

"And no going down the Villa. KRO. SOTV."

"The fuck?"

It's going to be a long holiday for the Sicilian.

## Notes and observations

- Adrien Brody is channelling Brando's Don Corleone and none too subtly but it's a stirring performance nonetheless.

- "Where's John do you think, Tom?" Well, here's a clue – it's got nine circles and a fiery pit.

- "I could fight a fucking tree and knock it out, Mr Shelby." Impressive stupidity from the Gold kid. He'll definitely fit in around here.

- "I heard you dress well, Mr Shelby. But now I see not so well as me." Mate, he gets more trim by accident than you get on purpose. Who gives a fuck who dresses better you anteater looking cocksmoker?

- Linda is not really a dyed in the wool Shelby so Sergeant Moss leaving the information about the intelligence service being after Ada might not be his wisest move. Will she even pass it on?

# Series 4 Episode 3 | Oranges are not the only fruit

**Strike the bloodclaat**

As we begin, Tommoi and Arthur welcome a brigade of starving scabs into the factory. They'd rather like to feed their families some time this century and so have decided to cross the picket line for some of that honest day's pay for an honest day's work action they keep hearing about. It causes some trouble among the striking workers so Arthur drags one of them out and beats him senseless. The older Shelby brother may be many things, unpredictable is not one of them.

**Mommy issues**

There is a bit of a turn up at the hospital where Michael's fake mom rolls up, having heard about his shooting in the newspaper. The boy is showing good signs of recovery and, given that he is at something of a crossroads in his life, the timing is fascinating. Despite being a fake mom, she's an infinitely better parent than Shit Polly with an infinitely better Birmingham accent. She offers him the chance to recuperate at her place, away from all the lethal violence.

"I know you got bored in the village but we loved you,"

She gives him some apples from their orchard. It's an act loaded with symbolism. Perhaps he might one day eat from the apple of non-shit parenting again? It would make a refreshing change. He is sad to learn that his fake pops is dead. Fake mom is all alone and could do with the company. He is quite committed to his Shelby life right now but the lure of village life is something Michael can seriously see the upside to.

**Bullet points**

For now though, fake mammy needs to GTFO as there's a Shelby family meeting in Michael's hospital room. Albert is a notable absentee as he is finally getting a ride off Linda on the office table. They manage to struggle on without his intellectual heft.

Polly is reinstated as treasurer of the family business which is really just a rubberstamping exercise. The real business revolves around photos Polly has got her hands on of a Birmingham wedding a few years back where Luca Changretta was best man. The group photo shows a collection of gully looking Sicilian gentleman, many of whom it is reasonable to assume are currently tasked with their imminent murders. So it might behove them to learn their faces yeah, maybe circulate them with the promise of a reward for information?

Also, and this is where the presence of Arthur would actually be useful, Tommoi and Polly agree that the notion of the eldest son sticking a bullet through Luca Changretta's noggin is impractical and regressive. Basically, the first cunt who gets the chance is the Chosen One as far as killing that guinea piece of shit is concerned. Aberama Gold is the strong favourite to claim that prize. It's a unanimous vote in favour (one absentee).

## Painting yourself into a corner

That notable absentee is having a busy morning. Having had his balls drained by his missus, he gets into it with some striking workers who vandalise the foundry factory with red paint. The nerve! The scuffle that follows is exactly as brief and decisive as you anticipate.

"Fuck you and fuck your revolution!" says Arthur.

Hey, don't let Ada hear you say that. You could be in for some real trouble!

Yeah, about that real trouble. A couple of Italian assassins choose that very moment to walk in and start licking off shots at Arthur. Seems like no one's respecting family hierarchy these days. Our boy takes out the first with a stray lump hammer, icing the second with the other one's revolver. That's actually pretty fucking good work considering he was outnumbered, unarmed and colossally stupid. He could keep the other guy alive to torture for information but, as previously discussed, Arthur is not very bright and he drowns him in a tub of paint instead. If this is a commentary on Renaissance art he's keeping it very quiet.

## My name is Luca, I live on the second floor

In the murderers' suite at the Inkberrow Hotel, Stratford-upon-Avon Luca Changretta mulls over his business. He knows that his assassination attempt on Arthur has failed and that two Sicilian mothers will be grieving tonight when they hear the news. Two of his lieutenants arrive. This Matteo character makes it his first act to complain about the terrible food in England. After being violently force fed some scones by Changretta though he seems to really quite warm to English cuisine. It's funny how things work out.

Take that old twat who got the hump with Arthur for beating her son to death during sparring in season one. The guineas have unearthed her and aim to use her to get to Arthur.

"She says he's crazy in the head," says the other Italian mush.

Crazy in the head is the worst place to be crazy in my experience. If she were to ask one of the brothers to come to her house, they would certainly oblige. Changretta definitely likes the sound of that. A plan is put in motion.

**Waifu for laifu**

As it so happens two of the brothers are having an emotional reunion that very moment. Tommoi is emotional because Arthur missed the family meeting and didn't get word to them that he was alive and well. Arthur's emotional having just plugged two Ities and had his first sex in months. Well, that and the news he got from Ada that his treasured vengeance against Luca Changretta had been taken from him in a democratic vote. The indignity of it all!

He's not making a lot of sense but Arthur does let Tommoi know that the Italians came through the back door. You know the one – the always locked and bolted one. So someone gave him up. There's a snake in the Shelby camp. Maybe you'd want to look into that, eh Tom?

He's on a real roll is Arthur. He may be a drunken oaf with limited self-knowledge and non-existent credibility but he has figured out that the ride he got from Linda earlier was initiated by Polly – a ploy to keep Arthur away from the meeting and the vote. Linda tries to pull the pussy card again but he lets her know that him killing Changretta is a non-negotiable in their marriage. Ah well, she tried.

## Picking the same scab for years

There have been some exciting developments in the search for the traitor. Tommoi has got Devlin in his office.

"Was it fear or hatred?" he asks.

It is an ambiguous one but he's happy to expand. Was it fear of the Changretta mob or hatred of the Shelby crew that led Devlin to give up his brother? There's a single ticket to Glasgow in Devlin's jacket pocket, which looks very much like inculpatory evidence. Men like Tommoi Shelby do due diligence and he has the address of the family Devlin moved to Glasgow a few days ago. The razor gangs will be paying them a visit shortly if Tommoi wills it and when it comes to people who set up his brother's assassination he can be very wilful. Devlin doesn't like the sound of that at all.

It turns out though that he's mainly concerned about the scab labour he is having to work with. He gets spat at in the street. Even a hovel like Glasgow is more appealing. It kind of rings true. Devlin is just not the treacherous kind. He tells his boss that of all Tommoi's many enemies his money would be on the communists for this particular outrage.

## Old flames never die (until they do)

It makes you think. One of those reds was in Tommoi's office just the other day. Perhaps he might pay her a visit? As he arrives, Jessie Eden is knocking back stout and listening to Blackbird on her gramophone. Single girl problems, right?

He's got a proposal for her but first he'd like to talk politics. As a member of the Stechford Communist Party did she happen to see two greasy Italians attend their recent meeting? Tommoi pulls out his Special Constable badge to show his bona fides (they really do dish those out to anyone like arts degrees and OBEs).

Over a beer they discuss an old mutual acquaintance. A pal of hers Kitty was the sister of Greta De Rossi, an old banger of Tommoi's before the war. Italian parents as it happens. Tommoi stayed by her bedside for three months as she died of consumption like a fucking Brontë sister. Kitty remembered a young Communist firebrand by the name of Tommoi Shelby. Any relation to the man sat opposite her by any chance?

As luck would have it, Tommoi has been doing some research of his own. He's heard that Jessie's sweetheart came back from the trenches of Passchendaele shellshocked to within an inch of his sanity and wound up killing himself like a little bitch. So it looks like these two both have their own issues with relationships, commitment and life-changing trauma. Shared sadness doesn't help them with their labour disputes. She's not fingering any communists from the wedding photo and he's not paying a living wage. The sexual tension may have risen but prospects of a favourable resolution have not.

She does bung him a photo of him and Greta at Blackpool before the war, which naturally enough sets him off moping again. He gets a bit of good news the following morning though when Arthur heeds the advice of Linda and fires the bullet with Luca Changretta's name on it into a 3000 gallon tank of shit.

"It's the modern way," he acknowledges tearfully.

Looks like the power of Linda's pum-pum held sway after all. She's so delighted with herself that she immediately installs herself as a bookmaker's clerk down at the Blinders' betting operation. Polly isn't too thrilled at the prospect but with Arthur and Tommoi backing Linda's play she'll have to lump it.

## Finn/Lizzie

More important issues beckon. Finn is still a virgin and for the family who fucks everyone this will not stand. Lizzie organises a hooker from Aston to take his cherry that very afternoon. Is there anyone who does more for the family than Lizzie with less reward?

Her good work for the day is not yet done. Tommoi takes her to the canals, like a true son of Birmingham, to reminisce about all the times he put his cock in Greta De Slutface there. It gives him a right boner and fortunately there's the loosest girl in Birmingham present to help him out with that. Lizzie Stark, the girl who put the anal into canal passes 35,000 lifetime shags on a freezing cold January afternoon with the unrequited love of her life. To call this girl a trooper is selling her way short.

## The Fredo

Luca Changretta was just earlier forcefully impressing upon his men the importance of fitting in when you're in a strange land. To this end, he's doing some sightseeing – visiting one of Birmingham's finest ancient ruins. It's Polly! She sips on a gin and tonic in Snobs as he approaches and a certain sparkle comes into her eyes. He's exactly the man she's been waiting for, with exactly the opportunity.

"The boy in the hospitals out of bounds. And I'd ask you to spare Finn and Arthur."

And Tommoi? He can kill that piece of shit all day. I think we just found out who the stool pigeon is. Polly was the Fredo all along! Fuuuuuuuuuuuuuck!

**Notes and observations**

- Jessie is all Shania Twain's 'That Don't Impress Me Much' when Tommoi pulls out his big badge but even a blind man can see she's intrigued.

- "Keep his balls empty and his belly full". Linda's mam's advice rings true down the ages.

- "People in this place hate forever, like Sicilians." If you've ever been to Small Heath you'll know that this is legit.

- "Spotted Dick – what is this? I don't want to eat that, why would I?" Matteo makes a fair point but when in Rome you do as the idiot English do, as his boss with the Roman nose forcefully tells him.

- Tommoi puts Lizzie in charge of his new charitable endeavours which should give her something to do in the 10 minutes a-day she doesn't have a cock in her mouth.

# Series 4 Episode 4 | Strike force heroes

**Mrs Ross**

In about 65 years' time, Goodfellas will let its audience know how your killers come with smiles. In that selfsame spirit, Mrs Ross arrives in Tommoi's office for a chat.

"Say, you remember that son of mine your boy Arthur beat to death four years ago? It would have been his 21st birthday tomorrow so we're having a bit of a shindig round and mine at noon. It would be just swell if Arthur could come along and GET WHAT'S COMING TO HIM."

"Sorry, what was that?"

"If Arthur could come along and help us celebrate! Nothing weird or anything. Absolutely above board and not suspicious."

"Sounds legit," says Tommoi, "I'll pass it on."

Despite this completely normal arrangement Tommoi has gotten it into his head that a trap is being set. In a series defined by psychotically vengeful mothers, you really can't be too careful. Countermeasures are taken. They set up an ambush on Navigation Street.

## Doing the ward rounds

Arthur shows up at Mrs Ross's at 12 on the dot. The mood may accurately be described as awkward. As she lets him know that she hasn't forgiven him (durr), moody Italians take up their positions on Navigation Street. Just wait – they won't know what's hit them! Everything is going according to plan.

And then the strangest thing happens. The Italians just drive away. It's almost as if getting Arthur to Mrs Ross's was a decoy to draw attention away from some other operation. Ah.

Over at the hospital Michael gets some unexpected visitors. It's Luca and his boys! The bodyguard is quickly iced and Luca can have a good chat with the Shelby Company Limited treasurer.

"Tell your mother, we have a deal."

I mean, you could have just told her yourself but OK bro. We will send the bodyguard's wife and three kids your sincere apologies yeah? I'm definitely not going to this hospital.

A sharp tool like Tommoi quickly figures out that Michael will be the target and it is to the hospital they speed. When he arrives, Michael neglects to tell him about the little chat he just had with Luca mainly because he doesn't know exactly what it meant. Polly in bed with the Italians? When you say it like that, it sounds all too plausible.

**Cunty roads, take me home**

Tommoi acts fast, leaping onto the blower to A Gold to set up a country roads ambush for the retreating Italians. One Luigi gets his throat cut, a local copper takes a slug in the arm and Changretta has to withstand some heavy gunfire before GTFO in the motor.

Once Michael gets some quality alone time with his mammy, he confronts her about the Italian stallion in her life.

"You agreed to give up Tommoi save my life."

"Oh well figured, shit for brains. Those private school fees were well spent, right enough."

"FFS, mom!"

You get the picture. Polly's murderous treachery doesn't sit well with Michael. Child sacrifice is so biblical.

But then Tommoi always did have something of the Old Testament about him. Observe now as the strides through the streets at night to do business with the turnip headed fuckwit Aberama Gold. For a man who just failed to assassinate his target he's very full of himself. Tommoi bungs him a few quid for icing the low rank Romans but has no problem telling him that when he has Changretta in his sights, that piece of shit is deader than the chances of a successfully out gay gypsy.

**May, maybe not**

Much more pleasant company awaits the following morning. Tommoi is discussing a certain filly who rides better than any in the land. But enough about Mrs Fitz-Carleton, by all accounts their horse goes like the clappers as well. May has decided to call her Dangerous after how she likes her men. She has come for his signature on some forms by which she means "his nuts" on "her chin". So trust that old skank Lizzie Stark to come in and run a monumental cockblock, talking trash about how Tommoi gets easily distracted by glamorous things, as if that's breaking news.

That's May's cue to GTFO of Birmingham and back to her £7m palace in London though that's gonna be a bit of a problem. The railway union have just called a wildcat strike, meaning May will be spending the night in the Midland

Hotel, sipping on Tommoi's gin and sucking on Tommoi's two-inch pecker if he is lucky. Organise your life in a certain way and the possibilities for joy are endless.

## In the family way

Back at the bookies, Polly is on the blower talking to a gentleman caller. Don't get excited – it's just that camel-nosed prick Changretta putting the shits up her.

"We will kill your son if you do not deliver Tommoi Shelby."

It puts her in a right tizz. She immediately wrangles Tommoi's diary out of Lizzie to set the date and time of his murder. It doesn't take much – just a bit of tea leaves reading is enough for Lizzie. She may be a cum sponge for the men of the Shelby family but everyone has their limits and with his recent pump-and-dump and brazenly sniffing around his horse lady, Tommoi just reached hers.

So Polly quickly makes a murder date for Tommoi on Friday and, having read Lizzie's leaves, declares that she is pregnant. A son and heir for Tommoi? Wait, doesn't he already have one of those? What a tangled web we weave when we put our cocks in many la-dies.

## Gym rats

The noble art of ritualised violence, though. That's always uncomplicated yeah? Tommoi and Aberama look over the young prospect as he spars. The civilising of the fledgling pug is going well.

"He works hard, he's game, I need to work on his defence" is the trainer's Mr Main's verdict.

It looks like he's ready for his pro debut. It's a real David against Goliath contest. Well, the opponent's name is Goliath at least. I did warn you about this getting Old Testament.

## Bus: stop

Over at the foundry, Devlin has to explain to Tommoi why there are no workers. He tells his boss that the strikers intercepted their bus and threatened their families, telling them that come the revolution, their names will be on lists, just like in Russia. Labour disputes! Tommoi puts in a quick phone call to the family communist Ada. This union agitating is ruining their respectable crime family endeavours. Sort it out, Ada. Jesus.

## How not to have sex

Once that's out of the way it's time to visit May and give her the spartan sex she so richly deserves. When he arrives she's already pissed on his shitty gin. FFS, May. Still, they walk around his bullshit distillery outfit and talk. She's not crazy about his gin but she is crazy about his cock and balls which, after all, is the reason she's there in the first place. Before you know it, it's suck face city. Things are getting hot and heavy right enough, but in the storied tradition of her kind May has to find a way not to have sex with him. In this instance, it's with a barely veiled critique of his business practices. RIP his boner. FFS, May.

Tommoi says he has something to show her. Will it be his cock and balls? He confesses that there is no wildcat strike. He only told her that so he could put his cock and balls in her. She doesn't say as much but she's clearly impressed by the lengths he went to. He dumps on the barge to Snow Hill to catch the 7:15 PM to London.

"That was some sweet aristocrat pussy and no mistake…" he says bitterly to himself as he waves goodbye. How did he manage to fuck that one up?

## It's my party

At the Stechford Communist Party, Jessie Eden rabble-rouses like a true soulless communist piece of shit. There on Shelby family business is Ada who buttonholes her right afterwards. It's about time these two ladies had a drink. And if they happen to lez off while the cameras are rolling, who are we to stop them?

Tommoi's terms seem remarkably generous. Parity between men and women established, the pay cut for men reversed and all he asks in return is for some Socialism 101 lessons from Jessie which she would probably have given him for free had he asked nicely. A dinner date in the steelworks factory is made. Who said war on three fronts had to be afflictive?

## Jew make me feel brand-new

Sounds like a Jew thing to me. On that note, who's this disgusting Hebrew exiting a motor in Small Heath? It's Alfie Solomons! Not saviour killing today? He's brought the aforementioned Goliath with him and, true to cliché, he's a gigantic turd - 7 foot if he's an inch.

When Tommoi and Alfie get to parlaying at the distillery, Alfie informs him that Sabini is still backing the Sicilians' play down in London. Alfie doesn't see much of a future for Tommoi but his old buddy asks him to consider the possibility that the devil he knows might be better than the Sicilians he don't. Because they will be heading for London once they've made mincemeat of the Shelbys and that's a problem both for him and Darby Sabini. He might want to pass that on to his old frenemy.

While this is undoubtedly food for thought for now boxing is the subject at hand. Aberama Gold enters chewing a decent sized portion of scenery he annexed on his way in. Tension between him and Alfie immediately rises as their two boxers are assessed. Somehow, Goliath is a welterweight despite being 400 stone and 90 feet tall. It doesn't bother the Traveller, though.

"Name the day, Mr Shelby."

Back in those days, the best fought the best.

**All must have prizes**

Just before his weekend begins, Tommoi has some business in the hospital with Michael. Just a few forms to sign, nothing major. He mentions how Polly wants him to go to the foundation for a prizegiving on Friday. Sounds like that will be awesome. Given the opportunity to say, I dunno, "It's a trap Tommoi, she's setting you up for certain death" Michael opts to keep his yap shut. Cousins are ten-a-penny but you only get one mam. Unless you're Michael who has two but - oh you know what I mean.

As Tommoi drives off, he is followed by a van filled with Changretta and numerous machine-gun wielding goons.

Organise your life in a certain way and the possibilities for despair are endless.

**Notes and observations**

- It's a big day for young Finn as Arthur shows him his first apartment. The broken glass, rats and stench of piss are the downside but the location is remarkable - Birmingham! Hoo-fucking-ray. The sensitive boy explains to Arthur how he is not a ruthless killer like the rest of the Shelby brothers and Arthur tells him he knows. Always time for that to change, mind.

- May signs a blank cheque to the Grace Shelby foundation and Lizzie makes sure she pays £10,000. Yeah well, the joke's on you Lizzie because May spends that on eyeliner in a month.

- "The man you're waiting for doesn't exist." Uncle Charlie to May in a rare display of ontological wisdom.

- "I see myself 40 years old having done fuck all except tramping the lanes. I see my life wasted. I won't let it happen." It looks like Bonnie Gold is set out to be a terrible disappointment to his father one way or the other

- "You bite like your horse." Let's leave the details of how May knows Dangerous the Wonder Horse's propensity for biting for another time, (preferably another lifetime).

# Series 4 Episode 5 | Industrial relations

## The Italian job (again)

"Shoot out his tyres," Changretta tells his men as Tommoi approaches Artillery Square. "He may attempt to surrender but it is I who must fire the final shot. Because in a Sicilian vendetta the man who-"

"Yeah all right fuckface, we've watched Godfather II."

Some of these provolones have got a right fucking mouth on them. In any event, they jump out of the van, guns cocked ready to put a hurting on the Blinders kingpin. Is it ogre for Tommoi?

Call it a sixth sense or perhaps the disgusting smell of salami but Tom has already sensed something is up. He is in the flats above the square waiting to pick them off with his gigantic gun from series one. One Italian drops before Tommoi's ammo runs out and he has to skedaddle. They give chase.

"He was prepared! That bitch lied to me!" says Changretta

Maybe. Further gunplay follows as they hurtle around the tenements. Tommoi drops three Italians before the cops arrive to break it up.

## We are family

You know what that means – it's time for a family meeting! All the gang are there – Arthur, his shit wife, Polly, that other one. Tommoi and Polly reveal that her betrayal was part of their master plan all along. As a coke snorting Arthur struggles to deal with being kept out of the loop for the 493rd time since the show began, Lizzie looks at her baby father and wonders when would be a good time to give him the good news about his child growing in her womb among the HPV and chlamydia. The left-field answer turns out to be "right fucking now".

"It's OK Tom," she assures him, "We'll be OK!"

"LOL! What you mean 'we' you horse faced old skank?"

FFS, Tommoi.

## Polly, amorous

With everyone lying low and the hospital having some shocking security issues, Polly brings Michael along to the Aberama Gold encampment where he learns he will be travelling with the Palmers and the Boswells from the 80s Scouser sitcom Bread for the foreseeable future.

"No fucking way," is his completely sensible response. Some things are worse than death and living with these humps is undoubtedly one of them. Nonetheless, his idiot mother persuades him that it is the best course of action for now. Harder to hit a moving target and all that.

While she's out, Polly finds time to go rabbit hunting with Aberama Gold. It's just the antidote she needs to being confined to Small Heath. It's not long before she's putting a knife to his throat and he's putting his cock in her foof. There is no love more foul, more risible, more offensive than old love but on the bright side at least we don't have to worry about Polly falling pregnant. The world's shittest mom has mommed for the last time.

**Camden Town**

How about we take a trip to Camden Town? Why not – the Italians are doing it. They pay a visit to Alfie. Not gonna lie, he's hard work.

"You're a bit of a failure aren't you? You come all the way over here to this country to kill Tommoi Shelby but – well, he's not dead is he?"

"Thanks for the recap, Shylock" says a clearly flustered Changretta.

It doesn't take a genius to figure out why Changretta is here, which is a good job because Alfie is assuredly no genius. Which is not to say that he doesn't have some Jew moves up his sleeve and yes, in his locker.

Naturally, he'll be willing to sell Tommoi out for the right price, like Judas before him. The place will be the boxing match in Birmingham between Bonnie Gold and Goliath. The price is an agreement to ship his rum into the Mafia's distribution network along with twelvty English pounds.

"You'll have to put on a hundred on top of that because you are a fucking wop, mate"

Like all of his kind, he drives a hard bargain. He insists that the Sicilians posing as Jewish seconds in Gold's corner be circumcised.

"I've heard of criminals paying for a tipoff but this is ridiculous!" cracks Changretta, to tumbleweed.

"No? Fuck you guys, seriously. So much for the legendary Yid sense of humour."

And lo, the deal is struck. And yet it kind of isn't. Because, as Alfie points out, Changretta has just made a deal without negotiation. Which means that he has no intention of honouring the deal and that, as Tommoi points out, he plans to kill them all like a vengeful Old Testament God sending plagues on the Egyptians.

Still, cross that bridge when we come to it yeah?

**Fight the power**

Meanwhile, in the Midlands the deep state come for that filthy communist Ada. She lands in front of Colonel Ben Younger, a mixed-race gentlemen which seems unlikely. She tries to explain that she is not down with the reds anymore. He explains to her that in these extraordinary volatile times a half-communist half-criminal could be very useful to the British state. Something to think on after he lets her go, as he does. Perhaps you might mention him to Tommoi when she next talks to him. It's a conversation that happens that very evening.

"Talk to me about Colonel Ben Younger."

It turns out that Younger worked under Tommoi in Flanders (no, not like that). The government has offered him three five-year contracts to supply military equipment to the British Army if he can get to the communists through Jessie Eden. So what Tommoi wants to know is will Ada be joining him in the counterrevolution or not? She'll get back to him on that.

## Table manners

The other lady in red in his life beckons. The date with destiny in the shape of Jessie Eden, arrives. She gets all her demands and in return he is hoping to get a rundown on the runners and riders of the godless communist scum currently ruining the country. Jessie's not a girl who really does that kind of thing and instead she tries to convert him back to the cause. There's a slow dance and make out but when he lunges in for a Donald Trump style fanny grab she balks.

"Soon," she promises.

"Arrange a meeting of the appropriate people and I'll be there," he tells her.

Oh, he's sorely tempted. But not that sorely tempted. Because the chances of Tommoi turning down millions in military contracts, pissing off the British government and putting himself in Churchill's rifle sights for the rest of his life for some communist piece of ass are remote.

## Fight or flight

As we finish, it's the night of the fight. Gold versus Goliath for the welterweight championship they just decided existed between 10 stone fighters and 300 lb freak shows. The punters are swarming through the doors. It looks like it's going to be an incredible event.

Yeah, and that may be the problem. Tommoi's Spidey senses are tingling. Like his colossal nause of an aunt he sees his own future. A camel-nosed prick looms very large in it. Look out, Tommoi!

**Notes and observations**

- Alfie spending 30 minutes a day with his eyes closed to better understand the blind is an intriguing character point. It's not one Luca Changretta particularly cares for but who asked him?

- Solomons has clearly not forgiven the Italians for all the racial abuse from a few years back. It takes a village to raise a racist.

- "If any harm comes to Michael you shall have me as your enemy and none of your knives can kill me." Polly, once again struggling with logic, the laws of physics and life in general.

- We appear to be getting back into government conspiracy territory with this Secret Agent Shelby business - Tommoi working the reds for the government. Your mileage will vary on whether or not this is a good thing.

- "I'm approaching the current political crisis as I would approach a horse race." What, you get your lunatic aunt to knife a rapey Prod as the punters are placing their bets? Not sure if Tommoi is going to be easy to pin down politically.

# Series 4 Episode 6 | The special relationship

## The bigger they come

Tommoi takes the opportunity of the abandoned dressing room to get some alone time. Unfortunately, he's shit out of luck because here comes Alfie Solomons with more of his signature bullshit philosophising. He tells him how he's going to sell up and move to Margate. Now the Americans are here it seems the savvy thing to do.

"Big fucks small," he explains, foreshadowing Jamie Cullum and Sophie Dahl by 90 years.

Let's see if that's the case with the big-vs-small contest in the ring, yeah? When the fight between Bonnie and Goliath begins, it's Rock 'Em Sock 'Em Robots. Both of these men are ready to go to war and sit in the pocket exchanging bombs.

Meanwhile, the ladies Polly, Lizzie and Ada are in the restroom catching up on the latest gossip. Top of the agenda is Lizzie giving birth to Ada's niece or nephew in eight months. A quick fondle of her tits and Polly announces that it will be a girl. God help the little bastard.

## Could it be tragic?

As the fight continues into the championship rounds, Arthur can't help but comment how the Goliath cornermen just don't look like fighting men. No boxing Jews these is his assessment.

"It's the pills and the booze spooking you Arthur," says Tommoi and right enough he's got through two crates of Diamond Blush and 4 grams of beak. Stupid Arthur. And get this, when one of the cornermen disappears off, Arthur follows him. Will he never learn?

As the fight reaches the climactic fix in the fourth round, Tommoi can't help but notice how the second Goliath cornerman goes for a wander. To lose one cornerman might be considered a misfortune, to lose two raises the appalling vista that Arthur was actually right about something. Tommoi sets out to investigate and Polly follows suit.

And Arthur? Well, there's good news and bad news. The good news is he's been proved right - there was an Italian conspiracy all along! The bad news is, he discovers this when he is garrotted by one of the Guidos. Although Tommoi arrives to slay the assassin, his brother's lifeless body slumped on the floor tells its own story. Tommoi looks over his stricken brother, tears welling up in his eyes. He looks a proper bag of shit. Plus ça change.

As Bonnie Gold finishes off Goliath in the fourth as instructed, a distraught Tommoi delivers the bad news to Polly and Linda that Arthur is no longer of this world. He may be no doctor but he knows a dead bag of shit when he sees one. He puts out the word. The surviving Italian gets blinded by Finn to really push the Peaky Blinders brand that apparently isn't striking the fear of God into people like it used to. The little prick looks like he's enjoying it a wee bit too much.

Like the grandstanding fuck he is Tommoi takes to the centre of the ring to give an impassioned speech about how his brother's death and how he's awfully sad about it. It is interrupted when Uncle Charlie comes into whisper something into his ear. The endgame for the Peaky Blinders is begun.

## Win with grace, lose with dignity

Arthur's funeral is a terribly sad day. Michael is called to Casa Shelby where Polly tells him of the change of plan. It's no longer Australia for him – it's New York. And he's going like right now. By Order of the Peaky Fucking Blinders

"You made a choice." says Tommoi, "You knew I was going to be shot and you chose not to tell me."

Bit harsh that, given the circumstances but OK. Exile it is for Michael like an Old Testament Jew.

Arthur's ceremony is essentially a rerun of John's. Gypsy caravan, petrol fuelled cremation, there's even another unwelcome Italian. It's that old bitch Mrs Changretta. She comes waving a white pair of long johns. Like most Italians throughout this century, she is surrendering.

It's safe to say that the sitdown between Audrey Changretta and Tommoi is tense.

"We say the vendetta is won. We will take everything you have, all your businesses signed over to us. You agree to this or my son will kill you all - one by one."

It doesn't look like there's much room for negotiation here. Tommoi swallows it as he must.

## Consolidating capitalism

Down in London, Changretta pays another visit to Alfie. Perhaps he wants to talk about all that anti-Italian hate speech? That will have to wait as Alfie has vacated the premises, leaving a booby-trapped door behind. Changretta is too slick for him though and spots the grenade just in time. Nothing stopping him taking over the operation now, which is very handy for him as that's kind of what he was going to do anyway.

Sunday will be a big day for him. He's coming to Birmingham to officially take over Shelby Company Ltd. It's incredible that the so-called tough guys so-called Peaky Blinders rolled over like little bitches just because two of the brothers were killed. It's almost unbelievable. What are they going to do about that, wonders Lizzie?

"We're going to let him have it," says Tom with the ambiguity that will one day cost Derek Bentley his life.

## The art of the deal

It's time for Tommoi to sip on the gin that eradicates seemingly incurable sadness. But wouldn't you know it that camel-nosed prick Changretta walks in just as he's about to get to it. He can't help but laugh at the pathetic sight in front of him. Tommoi, Polly and Finn – what a trio of rubes they are, standing there like little bitches in front of their shitty distillery ready to roll over and get rogered. Talk about a Kodak moment! Big fucks small. That's just how it is.

He's been thoughtful enough to provide a pen for Tommoi to sign everything over, though he will be insisting on him doing so on his knees, something Tommoi is happy to do. Because this is Tommoi Shelby, this is Birmingham and OF COURSE he has a plan B.

"A friend of mine once said 'big fucks small'," he begins. Shout out to Alfie!

Here's the thing. Two families in Brooklyn, want to take over the Changretta monopoly on bootlegging in the borough and Tommoi has been talking to both of them via intermediaries. Changretta dying in some bullshit vendetta in Birmingham, Alabama (the only Birmingham ignorant Yanks have ever heard of) would be very convenient for his Mafia rivals, avoiding a war between all the families while still taking over his operation. Perhaps that was the business Michael was sent to New York on? They've also been in touch with an up-and-coming hoodlum in the Chicago mob, Alphonse Capone.

Tommoi points out to Changretta that the blood relatives he brought over are all dead. The gunmen who stand behind him backing his play are actually now hired mercenaries of his sworn enemies. So while Tommoi is the one on his knees it is Changretta who's got the stiff cold cock of death in his mouth. A brief look over at his boy Matteo confirms the worst. As last minute reversals go it is rather splendid.

And like THAT it's on. A quick but memorable scuffle between Changretta and Tommoi is interrupted by Arthur, who looks pretty sprightly for a dead guy. Allow me to explain. When Tommoi discovered his older brother gravely wounded but very much alive, he had a brilliant idea. Convince the Italians that Arthur was dead making the Peaky Blinders' surrender that much more believable. Get Changretta to the table with his guard down and then get a bigger Big to fuck the Small that Changretta and his crew now unquestionably are.

I mean, he could have just killed him the 955 times he had the chance to but whatever. I suppose then, though the convention of the eldest brother avenging John's death couldn't be fully fulfilled. And that's what Dead Arthur is here to do right now. It a bullet to the noggin for Changretta and an ignoble death for the camel-nosed prick and one more funeral for his shithead mother who should really have stuck to teaching English rather than running her soppy mouth when she had no business to. His final act is to shit his pants in an unwitting tribute to Dead John.

300 barrels of English dry gin a month from the Peaky Blinders will be making their way to New York, further tightening their grip on organised crime in the city and keeping the speakeasies of New York wet as a Frisco seal. It is one of their more productive days.

**Dinner celebration**

Having finally returned to civilisation, they have a celebration shindig at Tommoi's mansion. Arthur gives a speech announcing that, despite his demise and official death, he will be sticking around for the foreseeable future. He strongly advises Tommoi to take a holiday now that all their enemies are dead. All work and all play and all that.

As focused on the prize as he is, Tommoi can see the sense in what his imbecile brother is saying. By strange coincidence he was just planning a trip to the seaside actually. Yeah, to Margate. To see a man about a dog. The man is Alfie Solomons, the dog is Cyril. Tommoi will need to find a home for Cyril after he kills Alfie for betraying him. It's always those annoying micro tasks that get you. This is why fiverr was invented. Alfie seems to be taking his imminent death well though that could have something to do with the terminal cancer gnawing away at his insides even as they speak.

In the end Tommoi kills the Jew just to stop him talking, taking a slug to the guts in return but nothing he can't shake off with a swift walk. Farewell Alfie. You kept it Hymie.

## Three months later

Fast forward a few months and Tommoi can't really get used to the leisurely lifestyle. In what passes for his mind, the golf course is a battlefield, fishing trips are a psychedelic hellhole and his evenings are blitzed by gin and regrets.

A combination of unspeakable trauma and supporting Birmingham City have finally got to him. A pep talk from Polly isn't much use – she just tells him how he should get used to the limbo that being a condemned Shelby entails. Tommoi finally figures out that it's the holiday that's the problem. Back to work he goes.

He gives Devlin his final instructions before he can leave and join his family in Glasgow. It is to deliver a message by hand to Jessie Eden. In it, he tells her the time has come for revolution – a revolution in his underpants, and she's invited. This is the best news she's had in ages. She rushes to be by his side. He wants the name and number of the head honcho so he can "help the revolution". She is happy to do that and later he helps her fanny no end by putting his cock in it repeatedly.

So of course, he immediately grasses the Soviet agent Casey Douglas to that old piece of shit Bigge in Westminster. He tells Biggie Smalls he is willing to rise through the ranks of the socialist movement and undermine it from within. And all he wants in return? To be elected Member of Parliament.

And so it comes to pass. Thomas Latchford Francis Shelby is elected Labour MP for Birmingham South with a majority of 39 million with Jessie Eden by his side and his bastard child in his arms. It's the corridors of power next for him. This is where things get really interesting.

## Notes and observations

- Radiohead's Pyramid Song from their laugh a minute 2001 effort Amnesiac plays during Tommoi's bad times.

- The look on Finn's face when Arthur reappears is priceless. It seems to say "I blinded that Italian for nothing?" to which the answer is an unequivocal yes. Effing Tommoi, man.

- "It helps me get through the fucking nightmare of being stuck in this city". Couple of things here. First off, Linda's got a right fucking mouth on her for a God-fearing woman. Second, as if you need cocaine to get through living in Birmingham! That's exactly the kind Brum shaming that gave the city a bad name for so long. That and it being a bit of a hovel.

- Peaky Blinders have now used up the one fake death that each show is permitted. You make a habit of this and everyone stops taking you seriously and each real death in the show is diminished. Don't do it again, lads.

- It looks like Matteo didn't forgive that scone business after all. Luca should have seen it coming. No one should be forced to eat scones.

**To the reader...**

Thank you for reading **Peaky Blinders: Series 1-4 Episode Guide.** If you like it, it would be ace if you could leave a review on Amazon. Your support is always appreciated. The author loves all you nerds and shares your belief in the transformative power of telly. All glory and honour is Hers, forever and ever.

God bless you all.

Other Aerial Telly episode guides you may enjoy at Amazon.

Printed in Poland
by Amazon Fulfillment
Poland Sp. z o.o., Wrocław